PRAISE

'This book is a comple
manual or a how-to boc
memoir – yet it contains   ....ing
I personally am very grate   .... think we need much more of
in this world. My advice to you if you've picked up this book? Let
reading Brighitta's words feel like listening to a beautiful piece of
music and surrender to the fact that reading this will be a Reiki
attunement in and of itself.'

Lisa Lister, Bestselling author of *Code Red, Love Your Lady
Landscape* and *Witch*

'Brighitta is a loving teacher who has made it her life's purpose
to help others heal and grow. *The Reiki Way* is a powerful yet
accessible guide that shares how we can bring this incredible
healing lineage into our everyday lives. This book is a treasure.'

Kyle Gray, Bestselling author of *Angel Prayers* and *Raise Your
Vibration*

'*The Reiki Way* is a unique Reiki book. Why? Because it is not
rehashing all the standard materials you see in so many Reiki
books these days. No, Brighitta is taking us on a journey like a
proper classical Zen book, so to speak. A journey of self-discovery,
of laying bare our True Self, who we essentially are. She does this
with beautiful poetic language and playfulness which nurtures your
soul. I felt a deep sense of peace and joy within myself as her words
seeped into my consciousness and nurtured my being. This book
is therefore not just for people who practise the system of Reiki,
but for everybody who would want to rediscover who they truly
are. Existing Reiki practitioners and teachers will find wonderful
teachings within these pages to deepen their own practice and the
way they teach. I highly recommend *The Reiki Way* to all who are
willing to take the journey to their True Self. Start reading and find
that spark within you, the spark of joy and insights.'

Frans Stiene, Founder of the International House of Reiki and
author of *The Inner Heart of Reiki*

'Brighitta is one of the most genuine people I know. She is an exemplary Reiki practitioner and teacher whose curiosity and extensive research gives us all a more in-depth insight into the great wisdom behind the system of Reiki. Through her words, knowledge and creative genius, she cultivates a timeless understanding of what universal energy is. This book is for wisdom-seekers and those that want to find their great bright light.'

Jasmin Harsono, Founder of Emerald + Tiger and author of *Self Reiki*

'This truly valuable book offers an array of amazing insights and reflections that go far beyond the usual description of Reiki as a complementary therapy. It shows Reiki as a way to realise deeper aspects of our being and includes fantastic meditations to explore this.'

Torsten A. Lange, Founder of The Reiki Academy and author of *Reiki Made Easy*

'I have been familiar with Brighitta's work and unique vibe for a few years now, and so to say I was excited to read this book is an understatement. Brighitta has found an alchemy that combines guidance, practical pointers and also rich and relevant anecdotes to arrive at a modern handbook for the spirit-seeker. I can see this being a well-thumbed favourite on my nightstand that I will return to again and again.'

Lucy Sheridan, Founder of Proof Coaching and author of *The Comparison Cure*

'Brighitta's kindness and passion for Reiki radiates through these pages. If you read this book you might just realise that the enlightenment you've been seeking is closer than you thought.'

Tamara Driessen, author of *Luna* and *The Crystal Code*

THE
REIKI WAY

Unlock Your Healing, Amplify Your Light
and Attune to Who You Truly Are

BRIGHITTA MOSER-CLARK

Copyright © 2021 Brighitta Moser-Clark

The moral right of the author has been asserted.

Apart from any fair dealing for the purposes of research or private study,
or criticism or review, as permitted under the Copyright, Designs and Patents
Act 1988, this publication may only be reproduced, stored or transmitted, in
any form or by any means, with the prior permission in writing of the
publishers, or in the case of reprographic reproduction in accordance with
the terms of licences issued by the Copyright Licensing Agency. Enquiries
concerning reproduction outside those terms should be sent to the publishers.

Matador
9 Priory Business Park,
Wistow Road, Kibworth Beauchamp,
Leicestershire. LE8 0RX
Tel: 0116 279 2299
Email: books@troubador.co.uk
Web: www.troubador.co.uk/matador
Twitter: @matadorbooks

ISBN 978 1 80046 266 3

British Library Cataloguing in Publication Data.
A catalogue record for this book is available from the British Library.

Printed and bound by CPI Group (UK) Ltd, Croydon, CR0 4YY
Typeset in 11pt Adobe Garamond Pro by Troubador Publishing Ltd, Leicester, UK

Matador is an imprint of Troubador Publishing Ltd

For your heart.

And to Matt and Eli and Anna,
who I love with all of mine.

CONTENTS

For the raindrop, joy is entering the river.

GHALIB

Foreword

I have been practising and teaching the system of Reiki around the world for over twenty years. It has brought me many insights and direct experiences, especially since I began training with priests in Japan to gain a direct understanding of Mikao Usui's teachings and how they are linked to the Japanese spiritual traditions of old. When I met Brighitta for the first time, during a Shinpiden Reiki III course I was giving in the UK, I noticed her inner spark was full of joy and insights. We laughed a lot during this workshop, as for me, healing and a spiritual practice is not always about being serious. A true spiritual practice is full of joy and playfulness, and yet we can be direct with our teachings and insights. I like this common bond Brighitta and I have, one in playfulness and a deep yearning for rediscovering our True Self with tools and teachings based on ancient Japanese philosophy and practices. This is why I fell in love with Brighitta's book, *The Reiki Way*.

The Reiki Way is a unique Reiki book.

Why?

Because it is not rehashing all the standard materials you see in so many Reiki books these days – hand positions, diagrams, historical stuff, etc… No, Brighitta is taking us on a journey like a proper classical Zen book, so to speak. A journey of self-discovery, of laying bare our True Self, who we essentially are. She does this in short sections which are written in a beautiful poetic language and playfulness which nurtures your soul. Reading through her book, I started to feel a deep sense of peace and joy within myself as her words seeped into my consciousness and nurtured my being. This book is therefore not just for people who practise the system of Reiki, but for everybody who would want to rediscover who they truly are. Existing Reiki practitioners and teachers will find wonderful teachings within these pages to deepen their own practice and the way they teach. I highly recommend *The Reiki Way* to all who are willing to take the way/journey to their True Self. Start reading and find that spark within you, the spark of joy and insights.

Frans Stiene
Author of *The Inner Heart of Reiki* and *Reiki Insights*

Introduction

My Invitation to You

This isn't a typical Reiki book. It doesn't include any information on healing others with your hands, or any diagrams of the techniques. Rather than create a manual that has been written many times before, I wanted to carve a path to the energy of Reiki itself – a non-conceptual realm of naturally healing energy where we can rest and nourish ourselves. Every living being in the Universe shares this common ancestor, and it continues to reside in every cell of existence – including you. You don't need to have ever studied Reiki or even heard of it before to enjoy this text, and if you never take a class that is perfectly fine too.

If you don't know much about Reiki, I invite you to sense it as an energetic inner space we can enter, rather than as a frequency we might occasionally channel. The space I'm referring to has been crowned with many names. The ancients called it the Pure Land, the Tao, the Atman. In modern language it's the Unified Field. I experience it as a deep, timeless dimension of inner vibrance. Every wave of the mysterious belongs to this ocean of consciousness we find ourselves bouncing along the surface of.

Reiki *is* primordial consciousness. The quantum enigma expressed as you and me. It's the milk we drink from the Cosmic Mother, the life-giving fluid within the womb of creation. It's the heart of the Universe. Reiki is She. The energy of the Goddess. Gaia. Shakti. The breath. Life-force. Soul. Innate intelligence. Source. The elements as one. The sage in the stars, the shaman within the Earth's dark caves. Reiki is the web that has no weaver. It comes from the unknowable realm where matter and energy are a continuum, where life is one lovely circular spectrum. It's the background container that holds the physical Universe, the river of conscious energy which flows through us all.

This is a transmission from the deepest recesses of my heart, from the place I call Reiki. This book will point you to this space, while the infused energy will activate your realisation of the awakened being you already are. This is an invitation for you to come home to yourself, a reminder of what you have *always* known: that you are the light of boundless space, intimately connected to all of life. You might find that as you read, a feeling washes over you; this is intentional and I encourage you to pause and enjoy your essence as it rises to meet you in these moments. You may want to have a journal nearby to catch any whispers that follow.

These pages are offered as a container for you to meet *you* – the being beyond limitations, transcendent of former pain as a keepsake of history. You are a being untouched by the past, an indescribable layering of vibration that exceeds our capacities of language. It is to the infinite realm of *who you are* that this book wishes to guide you towards. Back to your wholeness, with all of your humanity welcomed and embraced.

When I'm introducing a new group of students to Reiki, I begin by explaining that the gift of the practice is two-fold.

Though famous for healing, the true riches are discovered on its path of awakening. Healing happens all on its own when we connect to the intrinsic mystery within all of life. As we come back to our wholeness, we encounter healing as a potent elixir from our own soul. Just like Glinda the Good Witch reminded us, we had the power all along.

This is a no-strings invitation to come as you are. Everything here will be familiar, and it will tickle an awakening of what you already know within your being. It's about the energy of interconnection, the soul, life, the awakening of humanity and the great moment of healing we find ourselves alive in. This is offered as a guide into that warm attunement space of pure light, to help you find your way into your essence so you can become what you are. May it guide you the way a friend would if you were lost and couldn't see your way – by gently holding your hand and speaking softly to your heart. May it open the door so you can experience that delicious relief of homecoming. May we walk through it together.

Evocation of Your Soul

Do you know who you are?

Deep within the form you occupy, transcended of your identity, far beyond any thought or concept or narrative, do you know who you truly are?

Feel into this question for a moment and you may sink into a space of remembering... You are a nameless, deathless, formless consciousness temporarily disguised as human. You possess a name and a story, but you are neither of those things. Rather, you are the pure divine awareness underneath it all. The one that exists in the background, in the all-encompassing space between things.

We are all on this journey together. You and I are constantly evolving, becoming more and more of our true selves with every spiritual stretch mark. We are simultaneously different people with every breath we exhale, yet an internal aspect of us remains an unchanging spark of the divine. The true aim of the seeker is not to meet with a supreme deity beyond themselves, but to reunite with the inner light. What we long for is to find our centre, to experience a communion with our soul and enter our own power. With every metaphysical text we excitedly pluck off the virtual shelf, we hope to find our truth. We read words that point beneath the many veils we have in place which separate us from the rest of the Universe – but awakening remains a mere concept until we adopt the experience as our own. As each layer falls away, we find a closer intimacy with ourselves. Our inner light is of immeasurable brightness, acting as a beacon that calls us, and others, home. As our consciousness expands through awakening, so too does our reinvention, our recreations of our human experience. We reach for more of our True Self each time, waiting to find the life that fits, like a hermit crab longing for that elusive, perfect-fitting shell.

These words, and the pages that follow, cannot tell you *who* you are, yet they are pointers guiding you to take the most rewarding pilgrimage available on Earth: the inward journey into the infinite. This is an energetic voyage of remembrance, in which you may glimpse your True Self as far more profound than you've ever imagined.

We can all awaken to who we really are.

And my goodness, doesn't this world need us all doing our work! The time arrived long ago.

Soul-stice

I had one of those life-changing epiphanies on the summer solstice of 2015. My son was only two months old, and for the first time since his birth, I had ventured out without him for a little time to catch up with myself. I did what any new mother would do with this rare opportunity: I went to the park and lay down. Basking in sunlight, I nurtured myself with a Reiki treatment as I had done for many years. This was a simple and familiar activity of connecting to the Universe while gently placing my hands on my heart. I was on maternity leave as a photographer's assistant, a certain trajectory I'd invested in for more than half of my life, yet I knew my heart held no desire to work in the commercial world of photography. For me it lacked the very thing I cared the most about: soul.

As many artists do, I found myself on a parallel path supporting other creatives instead of *actually* creating, occupying a commercialised version of a very uncommercial dream. But this was all part of the magic that unfolded. The arrival of my son, Elias, whose name means 'ascended' or 'sun' depending on which Greek you ask, cracked my heart open and revealed all the truths I had so neatly tucked away from myself. I couldn't bear to miss a day of his fleeting infancy for a job I didn't absolutely love. So, as I lay there, wondering what future-me would be doing about her working life, I let myself be soothed by the warmth of Reiki. Communing with my soul, I went into the deepest place within my heart and asked a question that would prove to be a springboard into my true calling.

'What is my soul guiding me towards?'

Looking back, this was one of those perfect constellated alignments of life circumstance and body-mind-soul. The clear image arrived so pristinely, out of the depths of inner knowing, the way portraits used to emerge from the developer in darkrooms. It arrived fully formed yet completely unexpected – a sincere aha moment. At the same time, it was so obvious, I couldn't believe it hadn't occurred to me before. I arrived back home a mix of giddy, surprised and curious to tell my husband, who also found it such a familiar idea that it was strange it wasn't already my work.

What I saw was a simple picture of my hands, sharing Reiki with a client. From that precious seed grew my entire practice. Teaching arose without any real thought or consideration; I just followed the scent of it the way a wolf can trace the location of its pack through miles of wilderness. I had always been terrified of any sort of public speaking (even presenting my artwork to the smallest groups would have me shivering with the frostbite of fear), but my lack of questioning as to how this would all fit together kept my trail unobstructed. This might have been due to the sleep deprivation.

Since that wonderful moment, I have met thousands of beautiful people through Reiki. Teaching, sharing, practising – it is the energy of things coming together.

I listened to that voice, who naturally speaks to me in the language of images, and simply put one foot in front of the other – dreaming, creating and following its gentle guidance. Reiki was always the method I used to connect to it. And here it was, the way the voice had pointed towards. My baby had given me a reason to reach for my true calling, beyond my own joy.

> What magic awaits the one who lives this question as the quest: what is *your* soul guiding you towards?

The Seeker's Paradox

There is one message that has vibrated through the octaves of many voices. It has been echoing for aeons in every language, across all lands. A truth that all great spiritual teachers have shared: the kingdom of heaven is within you. One voice says: 'God dwells within you, as you.' Another chants: 'What you seek is seeking you.' You hear a harmonic that sings: 'All you need, you already have.'

Essentially, you hold the bell that will awaken the sleeping Buddha.

One tone in this choir will resonate, and you will realise that you have *always* held the key to your awakening. You will find it when you stop looking, that is the paradox. We hear this and imagine that we are looking for an actual key, one we've misplaced, if only we could remember where. I suppose it is a little like that; when we relax, they often reveal themselves, waiting for us where we passed them a hundred times, blinded by our frustrated looking. It's the effort that keeps them just out of reach – for what part of us is trying to awaken? The part that is convinced we are not yet there. All we need to do is relax into becoming who we already are, in this very moment. This has long been humanity's craving – the utmost spiritual ambition of any seeker. It's the seeking that caught us out, but it also invited the path towards the target. If we could just let go of the tunnel vision, we might begin to see the expansive vista of our highest fulfilment.

Connection is our truth. This is why the idea of separation is so painful, it's a lie. This illusion is why we have often struggled, as all of our relationships are experienced under the assertion of duality – me and you, me and that over there; in this case, perhaps 'that' is awakening – me and awakening. The chasm is a distortion; like an oasis we are thirsty for, it keeps what we seek just out of reach. Our language helps to reinforce these notions of separateness. If I am reaching forward in time to this supposed event which causes everlasting peace, believing it's going to be better than here, I'm never going to get there. The ticket to get there is to notice that I've already arrived.

When we look deeply at the seemingly dense level of form we live in, we find that we are oscillating atoms and waves inhabited by focused points of consciousness, connecting in a sea of energy and frequency. When we align our mind with this ultimate reality, we experience an awakening; we tap into Oneness and the infinite cosmic potential of the Universe. We bring the light of this knowing into our interactions, and this passive, yet radical action soothes the world. It brings peace. It washes away fear with waves of love. This is not just a theory, it is a universal truth. The way forward as a species is to remember and reconnect.

Once we are whole within ourselves, we can be whole as a planet and awaken together to an age of compassion and love; we can begin to live in an age where the pendulum swings towards our collective enlightenment. If we all understand explicitly that we are connected, then we might begin to take better care of each other and give more love to our planet. There is no one else quite like our precious Earth.

The aim of Reiki is to reveal our inherent connection, allowing us to tap into the deepest inner place – the source of infinite light in each of us. Your soul is already here. From that knowing there isn't any effort to bring light to the world, it simply pours out of your presence as you awaken to the light that you already are. In that alignment we feel the unlimited love of the Universe flowing through us like a river and we step into its graceful movement, letting it carry us. Once we've had this experience we can never really forget again. This is the distilled message of the many pages that follow and of the many years I have dialogued with the Universe: you have it all within yourself right now – your joy, your love, your answers, your truth. And just to reassure you of what you've always suspected: the key is in your back pocket.

The Way

Allow yourself to imagine the entirety of the Universe… It is far too vast for any of our minds to contain, but in the attempt, we pull ourselves open. We unzip our edges.

Reiki is a meditative practice that cultivates an awareness of the natural energy permeating the whole Universe. As we tune into this auspiciously vast field of interconnectedness, we become still enough to feel that we are one with the whole. Touching this internal space is transformational, deeply healing and activates an awakening of consciousness. When we connect to the Universe in this way, we become mindful of the deeper dimension of ourselves. We realise that we are expressions of the Universe. A being made of cosmic energy, alive in a world of frequency.

At first this system of healing that arrives with attunements can, on the surface, seem like we are connecting to something outside of ourselves, something new. But slowly we unravel that there is nothing outside. We are not working to channel an external force greater than ourselves; rather, we are becoming who we really are. The Great Bright Light within. The being that was here before it had a name, a body, a story of limitations and physicality. **You are Reiki**. The system provides a simple and profound practice of remembering that you are embodied soul energy.

By connecting to the universal intelligence, you can begin to feel the underlying web that is woven through all existence, heal your life and understand the deepest nature of your True Self. Rooted in Buddhist wisdom, this is a pathway of connecting to our inner medicine because it is a means of giving attention to our inner Buddha. This being lives in us all and heals with its very presence. It offers unconditional love and kindness, and sees clearly through compassionate eyes. This awakened inner being loves all it touches. Discovering this aspect of ourselves is the Reiki way – a lifelong journey.

What we find is the unconditioned energy of our expanded self, knowing how to receive the love that pulses from the beat of the Universe's heart. This is always available to us. We can touch the unseen force that animates, creates and harmonises all of life because it dwells in us. This one stream of consciousness manifests into infinite varieties of form. Reiki is an emanating magic that is rather indescribable, though it is fun to try.

It is not just 'spiritual energy' as a concept, it is the essence of the Universe that flows through all of life. The essence of ourselves. When we connect through our heart, we discover that our heart is connected to the heart of all things. Spiritual energy is all of the cosmic energy of the formless. We often see Spirit as separate from ourselves, so language points us in this direction even further, yet Spirit is All That Is – the quantum field of endless formlessness and the manifested form reading these words. This is a trapping of the world of duality; we see form and formless, yet in the ultimate realm where our soul dwells, we find that everything has energy and all of that is spiritual energy. Eastern cultures do not make a distinction between spiritual energy and natural energy; it is considered one and the same. That all-pervasive energy is what we call Reiki. Clients often describe it as a warm blanket because it is the blanket of immeasurable space unto which we all exist. It is the Pure Land. The canvas of spaciousness that holds the whole Universe. What could be more natural? What could be more spiritual? This energy *is* Source.

The great quest of us seekers is searching for this essence of ourselves, trying to get back to where we came from. As children, we were deeply in touch with our true nature. We took our time walking short distances, never fixated on the destination. We paused to wonder, to absorb our surroundings, curiously touching every leaf and new texture. We were in touch with our body and with our feelings, expressing ourselves freely moment to moment. In this human form you have lived the way you seek to live. Children are present, joyful, true, woke beings. We can get in touch with this freedom again. It was inside us all along – the infinite dwelling place of Source. This feeling sparks the healing, the change, the alignment with the divine. This is our wholeness, our fulfilment with the Buddha-mind, the soul, the perfection of emptiness. The peace we seek.

How very profound this work is; it seems as simple as the laying-on of hands but that is a small picture of the eternal place we touch. It begins with connection and goes as deep as our awareness will allow.

> Reiki comes from within you, the greatest
> you, the part that remembers not only
> where you came from, but who you are,
> right now. You are powerful. You are vast.

You are connected. You are unlimited,
unbound and unbreakable.

This is all so much more dynamic than a complementary therapy, though that is an undeniably beautiful and practical expression of it. Reiki is a deeply spiritual, holistic practice focusing on the wellbeing of the practitioner. Our practice evolves through our years of tenderly getting to know the energy. As our understanding of it broadens, it extends far beyond the time we set aside for personal hands-on healing. We practise Reiki with every breath.

I see Reiki as the energy of the soul in all its vastness, as a pinpoint of Source's infinite light woven through the great cosmic tapestry. It brings me home to my essence, as I focus on the deepest dimension of stillness within me while rooting my body-mind to the magic of the present moment. Any exchange with another is a gift that allows our understanding to overflow from our heart, cascading through our meridians to nurture both ourselves and the other. Together our souls co-express in this dance of energy. Where the mind had become fixated on a problem, the soul eases it into grace. As an anchor of presence in a world of frequent chaos, we invite order to return simply by joining the harmony of our unbound essence.

We don't need to figure anything out, try to control what is not ours to control, or aggressively assert healing; we choose instead to indulge in peace. The soul-voice is always whispering, guiding us to act with clarity. We trust that as we align with harmony, everything around us returns to its own natural state of balance. Healing becomes a way of seeing the world in its true nature, accepted and invited to be as it is. This includes anything we judged about ourselves in a less than forgiving light. I've come to see that the process of healing doesn't mean we need fixing or editing; rather, healing happens when we completely embrace every shunned aspect of ourselves. It's a journey to true wholeness. Reiki shows us that our mind is ultimately what receives healing in its perception of the world. We learn to accept and adapt; we water the seeds of compassion within our consciousness and we find a more meaningful connection to life by becoming friendly towards it (and ourselves).

The practice isn't unique to Reiki. It flows through countless teachers who bring the same quality of energy through their presence. I encounter Reiki everywhere. I've sat in the audience of Eckhart Tolle receiving what felt like an extended Reiki attunement simply by the clarity of his presence. Quantum physicists speak to me of it when they dreamily explain the Unified Field. It hums within Sanskrit texts. It chimes through every Buddhist monk's invitation of the bell. I find it in the Zen teachings, in the Tao Te Ching, in Animism and Paganism, in ancient Greek philosophy and even in a theologian's utterance of the holy spirit.

Reiki is everywhere.

Without being a religion, it is the basis of all spirituality.

This is one of the most remarkable things about Mikao Usui's method: he created a very practical, very approachable, yet very rich spiritual practice which requires no belief and yet provides limitless applications of universal energy through direct experience – from deep personal meditation to healing clients in hospital settings. Our focus is inward.

Whatever transpires on the external level simply can't compete with the treasure we discover within. These are the riches no one can take away and no one can give, yet they create wealth for us all. Others benefit as a natural occurrence – an offshoot of our practice. This flowering tree provides abundantly beyond ourselves. Our work is to nurture the tree, to root down into the earth, to open to receive sunlight and rain. The fruit comes without any strain.

The Mountain

In every version told of how Mikao Usui found Reiki, no matter which dramatisations were added to make the story more cinematic, there is one element that is always consistent. He awakened on a mountain. The perfect symbol for our journey, mountains are metaphors for the pilgrimage we make towards inner elevation. The summit represents a pinnacle of absolute consciousness, a space of divine inspiration whose height is made possible only because of its unparalleled groundedness. Like Reiki, mountains are synonymous with wisdom, stability, stillness, spirituality, purity, connection and nature. They provide a retreat for wise hermits in reflective seclusion, or act as an imposing force for many famous characters to overcome as they make great passages through the challenges of duality.

The climb we make appears transcendental, but when we take in the full panorama, we can see that we are arriving to our depths with every step. The mountain would be a flatland without the valley; we are as much that. *The Reiki Way* is a journey to find the sacred within (and all around), integrating our soul's energy while unashamedly embracing the full scope of our humanity. Connected, like the mountain, to the stability, pleasures and challenges of the Earth while touching the lightness of the vast atmosphere all at once.

On our journey together we will begin at the base, building a foundation with the fundamentals of the practice. As we make our ascent to the crown of these pages, we come closer to who we are, arriving to the ecstasy of ourselves as the unidentifiable essence. As we rise, we also dive into our depths, becoming familiar with the terrain of our vertical landscape as we encounter our True Self – the deepest, highest, timeless entity that exists beyond our identification with surface phenomena.

The kanji for mountain, 山, reminds me of Shiva's trident. It represents our life as a divine trinity: body, mind, soul; past, present, future; birth, life, death; mother, father, child; maiden, mother, crone; the cycles of sleeping, dreaming and awakening. The mountain has long been revered by ancient cultures as a cosmic axis, uniting heaven and Earth. This idea is reflected through our energy centres as we too are pillars connecting these seemingly distinct realms. The point of convergence is within the heart – a deep cave in the centre of the mountain where a river of pristine life-source flows.

Reiki is a spiralling path which traverses the entire mountain in all its deliciousness, a journey enhanced by our intrepid curiosity to go deeper into ourselves. Our steps weave through the infinite tapestry of our whole being. The mountain isn't here as a means of going somewhere else; instead it epitomises the totality of our aliveness in this very moment. Each bend is an opportunity to welcome our humanity, revisiting our path from another angle as we embody the wholeness of who we truly are. Rather than aim towards a future state of holistic radiance, exemplified by the summit, our *way* is an ever-shifting destination of our continual arrival, each moment vanishing just as it manifests without any desire to be anything other than what it is.

Chapter 1

Awakening
Light

The Universe in Your Veins

I believe our soul's purpose is to awaken to itself while alive in a body. To peer beyond the illusion of form while expressed in a world of duality.

> There is nothing we need to do to fulfil
> our reason for being here. *Being here*
> is the whole point.

We reach for this truth within our very own heart – the open expanse in the centre of our energetic being. The Universe is infinite in every direction from wherever it's measured by the perceiver. That's you, right where you are. And since your heart is your centre, it also happens to be the centre of your entire Universe.

Be very still, go there and feel the totality of the cosmos pulsing in your veins.

True Naked Self

As soon as we give something a name, we take away its true meaning. To see the world as merely a collection of concepts (that's an oak tree, this is an apple, there's a poodle), we lose out on the much deeper experience of connecting beyond the intellect. There is a deeper essence of life emanating from nature that was very much alive before we named any of it. By giving the energy of Reiki its own name, we create a distance between the Universe and ourselves. Instead of the essence of who we really are, Reiki becomes a thing from out there. It's often described as energy 'from the Universe' as if the Universe is somewhere other than here. But no matter what we call it, or how complicated anyone tries to make it, Reiki is us. Our true, naked, unborn Self. The soul. It opens the door to further expansion yet is everything expanded at once. This system should be taught simply, accessible for all and as easy to understand as mindfulness. It is a meditation. A profoundly minimal method of connecting to the Source within. Our inner Buddha. Awake, alive, compassionate and free.

The value of this practice is in our direct experience. There is nothing to believe, no concepts to get our heads around. The best teachers just point the way towards this cosmic river as it flows through all beings and invite us to dive in to feel the refreshing water of our own wisdom. Even if we don't understand it, even if we feel we don't deserve it, even if we tell ourselves it comes from this other more worthy place outside of ourselves, it is still ours. Who we are in our pure essence, flowing to meet us in our healing, acknowledging our inherent sacredness.

A journey to healing is a journey into Oneness. And a journey into Oneness is a journey into the depths of the True Self. As we make a reconnection to the ageless primordial consciousness some call Source, we find there is no bottom to the depths of who we are. We touch infinity.

Practical Magic: the System of Reiki

Reiki refers to the energy of the ageless primordial consciousness – or life's underlying intelligence – and to the system of Reiki that was developed by Mikao Usui in Japan during the 1920s. Through a magnificent realisation of deep truth, he received what we might call the first attunement from the Universe within his essence. His moment of awakening on Mount Kurama was an initiation.

He wanted to make awakening a practical sort of magic by creating a range of tools to meet us wherever we are on the journey. Today, most people will shorthand their description of Reiki as 'energy healing'. Although it is a wonderful gift to be able to adjust language to suit the audience you're speaking to, this really isn't the whole story; rather, it's the side-effect of the practice. Only by our direct experience can we possibly begin to understand. It takes us so much deeper and so much higher than our mind can interpret. This is a system of understanding our True Self. When we learn who we really are, we tap into the Source of all life to which we are always connected, and healing happens organically.

At its heart, Reiki is mindfulness. When we sit with ourselves, we can't help but become aware of our buried emotions, unhealthy thought patterns and unresolved pain. It gives us a chance to recognise all those places we need healing, and only in that recognition can the healing occur. Rather than run the other way, we sit and we look and we talk to our suffering. We invite our pain round for tea. Naturally what comes is healing, and what arises later is compassion. As we dive deeper into Usui's system of Reiki, we can't separate the healing from the awakening or the meditative aspects from the healing; everything is interwoven to give us this totality of the Reiki way. Isn't that the grace of Usui's design? Everything is connected.

Awareness is the first step in healing. We become conscious of the unconscious. In our willingness to be mindful, we open the door to transformation.

Rei translates to sacred, soul, spiritual, or infinite power. *Ki* means vitality, life-force, breath, the unseen energy that animates the physical world. The seemingly distinct pair of energies blend into one – the river of All That Is – and we experience non-duality. Connection. Reiki is the highest aspect of yourself, the one who is awake. The True Self. Your Buddha nature. The system of Reiki shows us that we are innately the Great Bright Light, and though we may have layers of egoic illusions that cause our suffering, we are ultimately free. We are as vast as the cosmos. The practice provides a union between our severed selves (human and being) and in this, we become whole again.

When I attune someone to Reiki, I am not bringing something foreign into their energy field from somewhere far away. I am simply reminding them of their truth energetically – holding them in Reiki as they wake up to an awareness of what is already within, so that they can access it again and again.

An attunement is a reminder that helps us to harmonise with the highest vibration of ourselves, held in that space of universal love. Rediscovering this vast dimension of inner peace is very healing. A hand reaches out to you as an extension of this knowing, from one soul to another. There isn't a conceptual framework that can be offered, it is a touch that communicates connection instead. An attunement is an empowerment to realise there is no self. Reiki is the purest energy of who you are. You are pure love; you are infinite light. You are made of the very essence of Source.

You are a spark of the eternal soul.

It is to be expected that we would begin by seeing this energy as separate from ourselves. Our model of the Universe is rendered in three dimensions as we live in our body in this very physical world. When Mikao Usui created the system of Reiki and gave this energy a name, it was from his enlightened perspective of non-duality. There was no boundary between him and this light that he saw as Reiki.

The Three Diamonds

In traditional Eastern medicine and energetic practices such as Reiki, martial arts and Qigong, the subtle body is primarily focused in three main tanden points (*tanden* meaning 'sea of energy' or 'elixir field'). These are known as the three diamonds.

Beloved Zen teacher Thich Nhat Hanh beautifully explains that there are three energies of the Buddha: concentration, mindfulness and insight. These energies are perfectly illustrated by the diamonds: our *hara* is a point of concentrated focus, our heart is the energy of mindfulness as it opens us to the abundant joy of the present moment, while the upper tanden opens to receive insights.

Rather than relate to the more personal journey of movement and liberation that we find in the chakras, the tanden points are our places of connection to the Earth, the heavens and Oneness. We are reminded that we are a microcosm of the Universe as we practise bringing awareness to these dynamic containers of energy. In Taoism these serve as sacred containers in which our energy is transformed – our inner alchemists. By working with the three diamonds as they relate to body, mind and soul, we begin to understand that the body was never meant to be transcended; rather, it is our precious experience of life in which to treasure. It is a vital aspect of our divine trinity and our anchor into present moment awareness.

Hara

Beginning with our foundation, we connect to our body and the Earth. We bring our awareness to the present moment and feel grounded, safe and alert. We are out of the head and rooted in our being. The lower tanden point is called the hara, often referred to in Eastern medicine as the golden stove. A few inches below the naval, this is where we store Ki – Earth-based energy. It's also the most sacred space of the womb. Through our naval we were connected to our mother, who links us to our ancestral energy and the lineage of all humankind. The hara is our centre of gravity, our powerhouse, our groundedness and the midpoint of the physical body. It's here, in this space, that our body converts food to life-force energy, taking the gifts of the Earth and creating fuel for our inner fire. This is the home of our original energy. Its themes are nature, flow, instinct, strength and presence.

Third Eye

The upper tanden is in the same space as the third eye, where intuition awakens as we connect to cosmic energy – the formless. In the highest expression, we no longer have mental concepts filling our mind, but live in joyful communion with the wisdom of life itself. The energy is often referenced as 'heavenly', but it could be seen as cosmic, or sky energy. The kanji for heaven and sky, 天, is the same – a stroke of Oneness as the roof above a human being who has arms outstretched. In many languages heaven and sky are the same word. This term doesn't denote a location, but rather a state of being aligned with clarity, vastness, openness, light and spaciousness. This space epitomises the serenity of a clear mind in harmony with the is-ness of life where we touch our pure, boundless consciousness.

Heart

The middle tanden point is the heart, or the crimson palace. This is a cauldron for the soul. It is where we feel our connection to all things. The heart is a portal where we enter Oneness, where there is no boundary between ourselves and the rest of existence. The heart holds our vulnerability, our courage, our humaneness. If the upper tanden is Sky Ki and the lower is Earth Ki, then our heart is the meeting point – the great everlasting horizon. In the heart, we experience the marriage of our two aspects. We are connected to the energy above and the energy below – as the great sanctuary of union between these two polarities. We are the sacred space where the energies coalesce.

Diamonds are valued for being the strongest natural substance on Earth (lower tanden). They have a brilliant clarity while light fills them with illuminating colour (upper tanden). They're shared as symbols of eternal love, representing divine union (middle tanden). They are the highest manifestation of perfection in the crystal realm. The three diamonds contain energies to harmonise, as a guide for balanced wellbeing – being grounded while clear and connected. Each container of energy is as valuable as the other, symbolising the beautiful, cyclical nature of human life. We perpetually move through cycles of grounding, connecting, expanding. This is mirrored in the three diamonds: Earth, Heart, Cosmos. We ground into our body, we connect to our soul and we expand with the whole mind of the Universe. One of the most treasured Buddhist scriptures, *The Diamond Sutra*, is said to be a teaching of wisdom so sharp it pierces through the veil of illusion. Absolute truth, once realised, is indestructible. As we bring awareness to the three diamonds, they serve as portals into ultimate reality.

Although we are balancing the seeming contrast between two streams of energy, we inevitably come to understand that each is an expression of life as one energy. Earth and heaven are two halves that make a whole. The Earth and the sky. The human and the being. The yin and the yang. One cannot exist without the other.

Ultimately, the diamonds serve as our points of connection. We plug into the Earth. We connect to our subtle essence. And we open our heart to receive the love that is our essential nature. More than anything else, we long for connection. We need it to feel safe. We are hard-wired biologically to depend on it. Each of these diamonds is a gateway into our sacred self. As we connect and align with our truth, we express our unique tone and bring the whole Universe closer to singing its true harmony.

We can use the affirmation 'I am connected' to help us when we've lost ourselves, but a truer statement is 'I am'.

I am.

I am.

I am.

Where does that statement bring you? Into your True Self. That deep *I* who *is*. A being who is one with everything. To say you are connected is a dilution of the truth; it implies that it's possible to be disconnected. Is the wave connected to the ocean?

It's the difference between saying, 'I am now connected to Reiki,' which is what we need at first, to saying the truer, 'I am Reiki.' I'm not giving my body Reiki with my hands; I am touching the space of Reiki that is already there. My awareness of it brings it to life. When we affirm, 'I am connected to Reiki,' what we are actually saying is, 'I am connected to the deepest dimension of myself.'

Going Inward

On your next breath, feel how your breath touches all three diamonds as it enters. Feel how the out breath is an outward expression of your radiance. Breathing in the Universe. Breathing out the Universe. We can use these points to connect deeply with our inner light and then to everything in existence.

Through our eyes, the Universe is perceiving itself. Through our ears, the Universe is listening to its harmonies. We are the witnesses through which the Universe becomes conscious of its glory, of its magnificence.

ALAN WATTS

The Symbols

Tools for Remembering

The symbols are one of the most commonly misunderstood elements in the system of Reiki. They have no special powers, they are not external tools and they are not meant to be treated as precious. They are reminders. Just as the entire system of Reiki is a reminder. A reminder of who we really are. A post-it note in your mind's eye as a shorthand pointer to a deep truth.

Blending Reiki with the sacred art of calligraphy, the symbols in their visual form create gestures of mindfulness, carving pathways for the flow of energy. As a mantra, they become tools for focus in meditation. The Japanese word for mantra is *jumon*, which means invocation, spell, magic word, or sacred chant. If you would like to try meditating with the mantra, you can repeat them in your mind to help you focus. The *kotodama* (sacred sounds) help us to harness another level altogether as we chant the symbol's vibration with our own bespoke sound healing instrument – our voice. Vowels are chanted to create a certain energetic frequency, the distilled mantra in its purest essence. *Kotodama* means 'the soul of language'. (Visit my website to chant along with me: www.the-reiki-way.com/extras)

The Reiki symbols tell us a story. When we are grounded and fully focused in the present, our mind opens harmoniously to our True Self; we realise we are connected to the entire Universe and discover that we are light. And are these tools for use in the external world, healing and attuning others? They are not; this is absolutely for our internal journey. These are tools to nurture the inner expansion that brings overfilling light from our very core outward to share. The Reiki journey always begins with this infinite inner realm, and from our enlightenment, we overflow to shine a torch for others.

Cho Ku Rei

The first symbol is Cho Ku Rei. In the Japanese tradition it is simply called Symbol 1, but in the West it is frequently called the power symbol, which is where the confusion comes from. The mantra (Cho Ku Rei) translates to Buddha consciousness, emptiness and spiritual energy. It is commonly believed that Usui created the visual aspect of this one, but it originates from an old cursive form of writing that was used by monks for shorthand that means 'go to your essence'. Your essence is where your power lies. When we focus in the present moment with our mind emptied of past and future distractions, our power unlocks. Our true essence only ever exists in the present moment. Meditating on this symbol doesn't bring power to us from some inconceivable place; it brings our mind to focus within the seat of our energy. Chanting the mantra with the mind planted into the hara can be very grounding as we begin to align with the energy of the Earth.

If it could speak it would say:

'You are divine consciousness embodied. You are in this body as a divine being. Come deeper into the body to encounter yourself. Empty your mind and remember your

essence. You are divine. You are your most powerful when you are deeply embodied. Bring your mind to focus on your essential life-force.'

Sei HeKi

The second symbol is Sei HeKi.

'Your truth is compassion, kindness, love, forgiveness. Remember you are infinite light.'

We have a bad habit of judging conditions as good or bad. When we soften our mind, we harmonise to the way things are and see balance. Sei HeKi invites us to tap into the unlimited bliss of our soul, so we can align with our soul's joy for life itself. This alignment quiets the mind and relaxes any tension. The message of Sei HeKi is unconditional joy; we are reminded to look within for our happiness rather than to reach outside of ourselves to satisfy our craving with food, drugs, or another's love. Joy arises from our essence. The symbols are taught on Reiki 2 (the practitioner level), which in Japanese is called *Okuden* – the inner teachings. We are using these tools to go within, to find the peace and joy that emanates from our True Self.

Hon Sha Ze Sho Nen

The third symbol is very profound – Hon Sha Ze Sho Nen.

'Remember your true nature. You are infinite boundless consciousness. You are the Universe. Your origins are right mind. Remember your heart is connected to the heart of All That Is. Remember your ancestry as the offspring of

minerals, vegetables, animals and consciousness. You are a child of the stars. Awaken to the true reality of unbreakable connection. The entire Universe is alive in you.'

We are connected to all things, all times. This wisdom is already deeply within us, not as a concept but as a visceral truth. In remembering our inherent connection with the Universe, we realise we are already interconnected to everything within it. The idea of it being a 'distant Reiki' symbol as often taught in the West is a rather shallow misunderstanding of the deeper meanings behind it, but remains a stepping stone into realising the ultimate truth which it points to.

Dai KoMyo

The fourth symbol is Dai KoMyo. The Great Bright Light.

'You are rooted in light. You have arisen from light. You are the Guardian of Light.'

Komyo exists in me and I exist in Komyo – the Great Bright Light is within me and I am within it. In traditional Japanese, Komyo can translate to the light of the Buddha. In other more esoteric traditions, it is linked to Dainichi Nyorai, the Cosmic Buddha. He is often pictured with his hand in the mudra of the six elements (or mudra of supreme wisdom) establishing the inherent connection in all things. The tradition in many Eastern practices isn't to pray to a Buddha as an external benevolence, but to ask the Buddha to join you in meditation so you can integrate and awaken their qualities in yourself. We contain the seeds for enlightenment, the seeds of compassion, the seeds of courage, and we meditate on the symbols to water them. The fourth symbol is a representation of our cosmic nature, the essence of the Universe, and our True Self. It is the emanation of Source that shines through our truest essence. The purifying light of pure consciousness burns away all illusion.

Going Inward

To use the mantra in meditation, sit comfortably and bring your awareness to your breath. Close your eyes and use whichever mantra you feel most drawn to. I like to imagine the mantra is like a raft; as I repeat it over and over to myself it helps me to let go of the struggle of swimming out to my depths. Eventually I can release the raft and float on my own.

Cho Ku Rei is wonderful when we need to feel grounded, and I invite you to focus on your hara as you work with this one, to help you come out of the head and into the body. This will help you reconnect to the stability of Mama Earth.

Sei HeKi is beautiful when you feel lost or out of harmony with the Universe. As it connects you to the qualities of the Buddha of Infinite Light (compassion, grace, love, heavenly energy) you can notice a tangible peace, like the stillness of a starry sky. Focus on your third eye for this one.

Hon Sha Ze Sho Nen is your mantra if you want to connect deeply with yourself. This one is for the heart. It can feel profound to place your hands on your heart as you use this mantra, either with your inner voice or allowing your actual voice to vibrate through your chest.

Choose *Dai Komyo* to feel like you are a giant luminous sphere. This one is particularly purifying. Instead of needing protection, if you feel you've come out of yourself and are noticing a denser vibration nearby, you can practise this to bring your light powerfully through your entire auric field, burning away all that is illusory. This is a potent practice to feel empowered, aligned and in perfect synch with your soul. Allow your mind to move down from your third eye, through your heart and into your hara. Breathing in, follow the breath down into your deep belly and feel your mind sink into this space of energy. As you breathe out feel the energy expand out of your hara as pure light. Bring the mantra into the breath and meditate for as long as you like.

Earth Ki: Gateway to Presence

The token emblem for Earth energy is found in the kanji for Ki, 氣 – rice, surrounded by steam. Rice symbolises abundance, nourishment and sustenance as the staple food for more than half of the world. Hidden behind this image is fire. The stronger the fire, the more purifying or alchemising it will be. In every tradition we focus on a strong inner fire – from Shamanism to Buddhism to Christianity. Fire is the yang element, while water is the yin. In the picture of Ki, we see the alchemy of fire, earth, air and water. We see the dance of yin and yang. The fire lifts the water so it can transcend its earth-bound state and rise to the air. The Earth is constantly changing as she moves through cycle after cycle, age after age, incarnation after incarnation. Her only true constant is the dance of her elements as they rearrange themselves. Our highest expression is realised when all these elements are dancing in harmony within us.

Rei is water – the most transcendent, most feminine element as it changes from solid to liquid to vapour and back again. Rei is the rain. The cooling nourishment that falls from the sky. When a drop of rain touches your cheek, a part of the sky has fallen to kiss you. An ocean rose to great heights to express itself as that raindrop. The kanji for Reiki is about the natural cycle of life as rain moves to the Earth and becomes vapour, returning to the heavens. This speaks to the eternal up and down movement of Ki – a wheel of energy perpetually turning.

Going Inward

Breathe your soul down to touch your body, landing your focus in the hara. Home to your powerful centre. Be solid like a mountain by building a strong foundation as a truly embodied soul. Full of your True Self. Build your inner fire here, allowing the vapour of your essence to rise back through your body to meet the great beyond.

As you breathe in, imagine that all of your mental energy is a ball of light near the crown of your head. Breathe that ball down into the depths of your belly. As you breathe out, feel your energy expand from the hara through your auric field. Do this for several breaths to feel both expanded yet completely grounded into your body.

Mother Earth is our teacher. We can witness her magic, her ever-cyclic nature. She is the most creative majesty. As we root deeper into her, we can truly experience this world as heaven. What a miracle it is to live here. Through her, we are blessed with the divine gift of life. Earth energy isn't limited to the planet itself; it includes everything alive upon her. The birds. The flowers. Trees. You and me. We all belong to nature as a source of life that animates us all. The belly of the Earth is where we lie, grow and meet ourselves. Our belly is where we can ground into her, while rooting into our own presence. The Earth and our hara (or womb) are concentrations of life-force energy, able to create fully formed manifestations (whether a child or a creation that is born with its own *kami*, its own spirit – like a book, business, or artwork). The deeper we anchor into the Earth's abundance, the deeper we know this as a truth of life. Her strength is our own. Her creativity is our own. Her health is our own. Our energy is hers, given to us without hesitation. Her core of fire is mirrored in ours. She's composed of quartz and iron – and we too have crystalline bones and iron-rich blood. We share the fire within our bellies. The wind of our breath. The water of our blood.

We have come to a crucial time for our species. Our ancestors worshipped this land and held a deep reverence for her that inspired ancient religion, healing ceremonies and a grounded purpose. If we are to continue thriving here, it is essential that we fall madly in love with our mother again. We must hold the same deep respect for her that our ancestors did. The way to her heart is through our bellies – through the ancient umbilical cord of the hara that connects us to our humanity, our ancestors, our natural world, our Earth. To deny our lower energy centres is to deny the sacredness of the body. Though our culture worships the mind and its technological advances, we can come into our bodies to feel the rightness of reconnecting – of working towards a common wholeness with our world. Through our heart we can feel into the solutions – the marriage of the head and the deep ancient wisdom we hold in our collective belly. It's here we can birth our New Earth, together.

There is no difference between healing ourselves and healing the Earth.

THICH NHAT HANH

Sky Ki: Gateway to Insight

There could be nothing sweeter than being alive while rooted deeply in beingness. To be in the moment, free of the mind's tale, like an open canvas receiving the entirety of existence at once.

When the mind is open like this, it is as vast as the great big sky. It embraces life as it is. It sees clearly.

The moment isn't judged, conceptualised, or miniaturised by narrative; rather, it is open-ended arising – ecstatic motion unbound by time or language.

Reflecting this expansive clarity is the deep lake of joy within our very being which captures the fullness of this moment in its limitless perfection. The soul dances upon it like light in spring, as it passes through new leaves. It caresses our heart with the sweetness of its pure luminosity and casts a prism of colour through our mind's eye.

The entire world unfolds right here, within us, arriving through our five physical senses along with the sixth – the non-physical intuitive mind. There isn't a world 'out there' since one hundred percent of it is perceived through us. And there is no way to prove this otherwise. Each of us is in a unique world of our own. We can't visit each other's worlds as it's impossible to leave the one we're on. The whole planet we occupy goes everywhere along with us, like a turtle who must always carry its shell, unable to inhabit another's.

> That which cannot be known is realised in the silent becoming.

Our divine perfection is what remains in the gentleness of the empty mind.

Where does the sky end and the cosmos begin?

Where does our soul end and the source of it begin?

Let us sit in the stillness of our mind on one of its cloudless nights, gazing at the whole Universe as we come to realise something precious. You are life. You do not possess one; rather, you are life itself. You are not your thoughts; you are the pure mind that contains them. The deep witness to it all. As vast as the great big sky. Feel this in your body using all six senses.

Going Inward

To connect to your vast Sky Ki, you simply need to come home to your breath. Our breath is the air that fills the sky above us and connects us to all of life. As we breathe into our body, we can feel the energy of the open sky touch our mind and our heart. As we expand the belly to breathe deeply, we welcome the energy of the heavens right into our body. We are embodied consciousness.

Many spiritual practices use incense to communicate with ancestors, evoking a sense of connection with the holy smoke that transcends the Earth as it travels up to the sky, carrying prayers to loved ones. If you'd like to try this, bring your awareness to your breath as you light some, invoking your love for your ancestors as you do so. Feel your connection. Receive the love that is there for you.

When the mind is pure, joy follows like a shadow that never leaves.

BUDDHA

Heart Ki: Gateway to Soul

There is a beautiful word in Japanese for the heart – *kokoro*. Its true meaning doesn't translate so well to English. It means the heart-mind. The union of the heart-mind-soul trinity. Not as three things that merge, as we might understand this in the West, but as one thing that was always just the one thing. That's the true heart, or rather, the right mind.

Maybe the brain is the home to mental activity, but if that's true where is the home of consciousness? It has no fixed point, no container. What else is like that? The Universe itself. Is consciousness the kokoro of the Universe? Are we the Universe's kokoro?

Where does your presence reside, is it limited to the body?

The kanji for kokoro looks like a winking smiley face: 心. It means heart, mind, spirit, inner strength and friend.

How do you touch the Universe? When you sit down, you sit with the Universe in its entirety. You can never be out of touch; you can never not be sitting with it.

The heart is the place I think we all decided to learn from in this incarnation, but in order to study from the inner temple of wisdom, first you will need to enter it. And then you need to sit, and listen, as a student. The heart is a bridge to our divine consciousness. The journey doesn't need to go beyond the realm of the inner heart because once you're there it will send you through the vortex of your soul into the field of infinite vastness. That's the quest, the journey, the guide and the answer all in one package. We don't need to ascend upwards, we need to journey deep within. We don't need to leave the sanctity of the body, it is through this vibrant delta of energetic streams that we can find our way. This is the gateway of kokoro.

My spirit is a flame. Does the fire do its transformational magic, or do I get burned denying it? Its light will guide me, but its ability to purify can make a smoke that blinds me if I don't focus on the brightness of that flame. We awaken because of a spark that lights our soul-fire. It could initially be reactive; this is the way nature has set the Universe up. Life creates challenges and suffering sparks the response of evolution. The soul-fire in the heart of humanity is burning bright. What gold will come of this time?

It's always been about the heart. The heart is the portal in and the vortex through which we encounter the world, encounter ourselves and encounter our souls. By its nature it is the space of coming together.

The whole point of Reiki is that there was only ever one energy, it just appeared as two from our conceptual perspective. The heart is where the two rivers meet the ocean. The mysterious horizon where Earth holds sky.

Going Inward

Try my Heart Grounding meditation at:
www.the-reiki-way.com/extras

You are the Supreme Being, and yet thinking yourself to be separate from it, you strive to become united with it. What is stranger than this?

RAMANA MAHARSHI

Reiki is the Soul of Life

Everything around us is Ki. Life-force energy. You can feel it, see it, know it within your entire body. Look down, look up, look in – it's everything. With our practice we can touch the Source of life's energy – the soul of the Universe. The very essence of everything.

Rei = Soul. Ki = Life.

Reiki is always there for us. Always available. This means that the soul of life itself is always here and available for us. It's accessible right now. You can reach into it whenever you like. You are never not touching the Universe. You are never alone.

The soul of this magnificent Universe is Source. This Universe is but one of its many incarnations and we are but one of its many breaths. 'Uni' means one, while 'verse' means to turn; from the Latin word it translates to 'whole'. As humans we are a small fraction of this turn, this revolution as the Universe. We are like cells moving through a body. The body of God.

Reiki is not separate from you, it is you – the Great Bright Light that you truly are, containing the love that is always there. Your eternal nature.

Going Inward

You can breathe up the Earth energy – connect to it with your mind and bring this strong concentration of life-force up your legs and into your hara. Feel the resonance.

Breathe down the Sky energy – feel the absolute vastness of space all around us. The canvas for the stars, the unbreakable stillness, the immeasurable spaciousness. Feel the infinite inside.

We can listen to the harmony of these universal wavelengths with their tangible vibration. When we journey into the heart of the Universe – which is our very own heart – we discover the instrument that creates this orchestra. We enter the central apex of All That Is. The hub of the wheel of life. Breathe into the core of your heart and connect to your Source.

Lineage of Light

Encountering the Japanese teachings for the first time, after many years of studying the Western, was like walking out of a cluttered home that was overly decorated and into a space that was meticulously planned with refreshing, minimalist design. Everything was clearly thought out, carefully placed, and anything not perfectly harmonious left out. Usui Reiki Ryoho, the traditional Japanese lineage, contains nothing to believe in. In its clear, simple, non-dogmatic approach it's very similar to Zen Buddhism.

The Western mind has a way of complicating things. The mind just loves to get involved, inviting in the ego and all of its trappings. When Reiki moved across the West, it filtered through a very different framework from its origin. In order to be successfully transplanted from Japan to America in the years just after Pearl Harbour (a naval base in Hawaii which suffered a surprise military attack by Japanese forces in 1941), the system of Reiki was stripped of its deep meditation practices and all its spiritual underpinnings, held up solely as a system of hands-on healing. What I love about the practice of Reiki is how simple it truly is. It's really just being mindful, concentrating on energy, accessing our infinite essence. Reiki promotes inner fulfilment, peace, mindfulness, compassion and love. The primordial consciousness – one mind, Source energy – doesn't require us to believe in it. It just is. Without being fancy or complicated. Just our true nature laid bare. We can access it whenever we like.

It's like the moon in the branding for my Reiki school, Awakening Light. Is Reiki like the moon? It is far more solar, actually. It's always shining, never moving through phases; it is so consistently unchanged. It's the Great Bright Light. Yet, to receive it, we must be like the moon. A receptive, luminous reflection of this non-stop light. In the Master symbol we have the kanji for the sun, 日, and for the moon, 月. Their one-light symbolising the unity of perceived polarity. So, our soul-light, Reiki itself, is the sun. This light freely shines upon our human aspect. We feel our best when we face the light. As it illuminates our potential and awakens our radiance, it then reflects outward, sharing our light without any effort. By acknowledging the sun of our soul and the moon of our humanity, we can simultaneously radiate and receive the light that we truly are.

Chapter 2

The Principles of Healing

The Reiki Principles

The Reiki principles can be found inscribed on Usui's memorial stone in Tokyo, written by his senior students a year after his passing:

Just for today

(Kyo dake wa)

Do not be angry

(Ikaru-na)

Do not worry

(Shinpai suna)

Be grateful

(Kansha shite)

Be true to your way and your being

(Gyō o hageme)

Be compassionate to yourself and others

(Hito ni shinsetsu ni)

These are a healing balm, a way to create deeper awareness within ourselves about all that we carry. The inner tone is expressed in a gentle grandmother's voice with soft, reassuring wisdom. We are encouraged to practise reciting these principles within our heart, every morning and every evening. If we have watered these seeds of awareness in our mind, then when anger arises, we will put out the fire with kindness. The guidance does not say we should suppress emotions; rather, it invites us to meet our emotions with compassion. No longer do we operate in the world unconsciously; we choose instead to heal ourselves. You may find that reciting them creates a purification process through your emotional body as they ventilate the corners of your mind.

Going Inward

Using your beautiful voice, which heals in its unique resonance, I invite you to chant them along with me in Japanese. (Visit my website for a video you can chant with: www.the-reiki-way. com/extras)

The principles are also called *precepts* – another word for instruction. By leaving us with the Reiki precepts, Mikao Usui was telling us how to go about using all the other tools in his system. They are the rich earth in which the rest of the practice grows. Notice how they don't focus on physical healing, but rather emphasise the importance of a healthy mind? Our mental state is the basis of every experience, the filter we see life through. Usui acknowledged the mind as the most vital aspect of our wellbeing.

It is said that his Buddhist students received a more elaborate instruction:

Do not bear anger, for anger is an illusion
Do not be worried, for fear is a distraction
Be true to your way and your being
Show compassion to yourself and others
Because this is the centre of Buddhahood

If we contemplate the precepts during meditation, they guide us to become the energy of Reiki – to embody the energy of the Buddha. We are guided to live as awakened beings who infuse what we do with compassion.

We can rest in kindness. Acting with compassion grants us access to a guilt-free conscience. In gratitude we make friends with life. We anchor into the present, and as we enjoy this beautiful moment we can reflect on past suffering and feel grateful for its contribution to our current experience. With an open heart we can recognise how essential each step of our journey has been. Gratitude sets us free. It gives way to generosity, an expression of our soul. The soul is at ease. It doesn't feel worry or anger.

Through the principles, we are guided to live as Reiki. To express the unlimited energy of our inner heart which occupies this very moment. It's in this space of stillness that we transcend the abstract conceptualisation of our connection to the Universe and feel the visceral truth of our intimacy with every particle of existence. In this vast space of our presence, all healing happens, all intuition arises, all inspiration arrives.

Your Feelings are Little Children

Your feelings are begging for your love. They want to be held, acknowledged. Not locked away and shunned. 'If you ignore me,' says the root of your worry, 'I will wake you up at night.' They want to be heard and held and healed of their wounds. Stressful thoughts have gravity. Emotions and more thoughts come to orbit them, and a whole universe of confusion is born. The principles allow us to sit with the first stressful belief and look at it, before the galaxy of suffering matures. Once thoughts are witnessed for what they are, they release us on their own.

The depth and breadth of the Reiki system is illustrated by the deceptively simple Reiki principles. The six little lines that I shared a few pages ago are a profoundly affective invocation to healing. They uproot our long-buried pain so it can once and for all be seen, understood, healed and released. The principles guide us to a deep awareness, so when a stressful thought arises, we can meet it with compassionate consciousness. We can stand firm in our light, so instead of hopelessly fighting the strong undercurrent in our emotional river, we sit on the bank watching the choppy water rush past.

Using them as an active meditation unearths the seed of our pain; this process will dig up anything that has taken root within you that is untrue. It might seem uncomfortable at first but watch as these simple little words burn away all that no longer serves you. Many people struggle with the first two pieces of instruction: do not be angry and do not worry. As soon as these words are said, the anger and the worry rise to greet the sentiment. As Frans Stiene (one of my dear teachers) so beautifully illustrates: if you are walking around with a cup of coffee and someone bumps into you, what's going to spill out of your cup? Not hot chocolate. That is the whole point. We are going to let the truth spill out.

Going Inward

To practise, sit with your hands together in Gassho (prayer mudra in front of your heart), which helps us to go within. In this gesture we can no longer 'do', we are just resting within our being. As you go through each principle, pause when one sparks a reaction. Say that one over and over to yourself, noticing what is rising.

For example, if I say 'do not worry' to myself, and I'm holding anxiety, I will most definitely begin feeling anxious as all of my suppressed thoughts come up to greet my awareness. As I see them, I keep going with 'do not worry' until I have let them all out of their hiding places. Now the thoughts are with me in my conscious mind, I can address them. I'm going to see them each as a small, innocent child who is asking for love and affection. I will invite each one to enter my heart and see if there is anything this little part of me needs as I do so. I will love all over my worry until it is seen and eased. I will tell it that I'll take care of whatever it is asking. Sometimes it asks me to listen to my intuition because there is a genuine cause for concern. I might have ignored it the day before. I'll hear it out. Then I will go to the next precept, 'be grateful', and I'll let the sweetness of gratitude soothe any residual energy the worry children left behind. This plants us so firmly in reality, it brings us to our truth and it activates our healing. Try this for yourself and see what happens. I'd encourage you to get your journal out too – it helps to take it out of the head and onto paper.

I often receive emails from students after a course, who have started to use the principles and now question the negatives. Usually they advise a rewording to make them more positive and suggest using 'be free from anger and worry' instead. This feels much nicer. And I totally agree that is much better feeling that way. Yet, if we make these into better feeling statements that don't provoke our reactivity, we are missing the alchemical response. Usui's golden path to uprooting buried pain. Reiki is a tool for emotional mindfulness, which means we become so incredibly aware of all the places we need healing and holding as soon as we begin to pay attention. The point is not to affirm that we are not angry. We are not trying to kid ourselves here.

We are not manifesting, we are liberating ourselves.

The point is to recognise all the places we hold anger so we can heal the destructive energy rather than keeping it politely stuffed down in the pockets of our body.

As we notice the anger rising, we are setting it free. Do not *be* angry isn't the same as do not *feel* anger. Feel it, but don't become unconscious to it, don't be consumed with rage and blinded by it. Use it as a call for compassion. So instead of feeling that 'I am angry' we give ourselves a chance to notice 'there is anger in me' and I am not it. Here it is, and I am here witnessing it. We can meet our emotions with kindness, treating them the way we'd treat a crying child. We investigate, we comfort, we embrace and hold space. We choose to see ourselves with eyes wide open. Once we've looked deeply into all our shadowy places, we understand what it is to be human. Our suffering isn't personal, it's universal. This gives us a new level of understanding for those around us.

Why are you here, anger? What do you want? Often this energy is rocket fuel, trying to get us to make some changes, and only when we listen to it will it stop creeping up on us while we're trying to live our lives. If you are not holding any anger, then the statement 'do not be angry' will not provoke anger. It is only provocative if healing is underway.

Our journeys to work things out for ourselves have an incredible ripple effect, through timelines, past lives, family patterns, conditioning – this is how we heal the world. We make peace in our own mind first. We learn so much about being human in the process. These statements provide a way to see clearly and be true to ourselves.

> Only in acknowledging our feelings can
> we let the feeling pass.

We don't shun, we don't bypass. We soften, allow, integrate. Heal.

Until you make the unconscious
conscious, it will direct your life and you
will call it fate.

CARL JUNG

Just for Today

Just for today is not a promise, it's a practice. The principles aren't a vow we take for life, they are just for today. We don't need to worry about tomorrow or get angry about yesterday. Our entire existence and the only thing we can ever manage is all happening in this current day. The first step in getting free is realising that we only have this moment. If we enter it the way we'd enter a room, we can take in everything the new space holds for us.

My son has a wonderful way of asking about time. Most nights he asks, 'Is today tomorrow? And is tomorrow today?' He knows that language is a slippery creature. He's learned that each day always unfolds as today, yet it is also a tomorrow and simultaneously a yesterday. It's all happening in the parameter of now. Yesterday is a phantom and tomorrow never comes; it's always today. Each second passes through the only moment we have ever had. This one. Now.

You are not your story.

You are not your pain, your past, or your Dark Ages. You do not need to excavate all your pain in order to release it. As you allow the healing to happen, the light shines where it needs to. Healing is our natural state; it is always happening, every minute of every day. It is so efficient when we no longer identify with our history, but rather release into who we have become. You write the narrative, yet you are not the narrative. You are the thinker, being thought.

You don't need to do anything to actively release the past. You just arrive here, in the present. Come home to life as it so beautifully is. Come home to you. Let every action you make be for the purpose of that action alone, rather than as a means of getting to the next thing.

Going Inward

If you can, right now, make yourself a cup of tea. When you pour water from the kettle into the mug, do it for the joy of watching the water stream down, notice how it enlarges the little bag, witness the steam, the cloud of colour erupting into the liquid. Gently place the kettle down with gratitude. When you lift the mug, be with that action completely. Then inhale the warmth as you lift it to your face, as if it's the very first cup of tea you've ever encountered. Enjoy every little moment of that process and discover how much joy awaits you in every moment of life. Your entire life can be lived like that. As simply and gracefully as noticing for the pleasure of it.

Be here with yourself, receiving yourself as your medicine.

Discover yourself as the gifted moment you find yourself inside of. Breathe. Move from your head to your heart and then keep going into your hara. Feel the rightness of your body. Sense the intelligence of life all around you. Notice the miracle of this moment.

The present is a gift.

Do Not Be Angry

Notice anger the way you'd notice a dog barking in the quiet night. The awareness of feeling anger is already a sign of awakening. You know you're not the barking dog. You can cultivate this awareness by resting firmly in observation. Notice that the true you isn't barking; rather, you are the alert one who listens. Often overlooked, our True Self has always been there. When anger erupts, we have a chance to notice who we are. If we are not the anger, who are we?

Usui's instruction not to 'be' angry isn't telling us not to *feel*. This is a call to wake up. To realise anger is not who we are.

The True Self is the witnessing presence,
always attentive, always available.

It is resting in the lap of our True Self that we feel at peace, even if there are ten dogs barking outside the window.

Listen to Your Anger

We can listen deeply to our emotion and sift for the gold in the fire. If you allow the alchemical process to unfold, you can use the heat of the flames to awaken from the illusionary mind. Tune in to the deeper messages being offered, rather than become enslaved by anger's hypnotic powers. Listen to your anger with curiosity. Look to find its underlying message. As we move to offer acceptance to the presence of this emotion, it softens ever so slightly. By giving permission to anger we create a space between ourselves and the emotion. Can you sense this space? Notice that the space could not exist if you were still identified as angry. When we identify as being angry, there isn't any space – there isn't any room for healing to flow.

Going Inward

If you feel anger as fight energy, is it trapped in your arms? Is it flight energy, moving through your legs and hips? Move these areas and shake the residual energy out. Dance or run or shake your body to move the intensity out of your nervous system. Then look for the creative solution from that same wise perspective that noticed the anger. Practised enough times, we eventually realise that we are impenetrable. Anger doesn't touch us. It's just something we witness from time to time.

What is the anger about? Really? Is it about what you have tolerated for a little too long? Is it asking for change? This force can be channelled like rocket fuel. It might prove to be the fiery torch of independence, asking you to begin a project just for you. Grab your journal and write through the flames. Maybe the change needed is in our perspective, maybe we haven't given ourselves permission to do something, or it might be stagnant energy. We can let that be a light to wake us up. We can choose to let it burn us, or to carry us towards a risen state. Instead of battling the inner dragon, can we ride it?

Approach the anger like you would a child in the middle of a tantrum – gently. Open your arms to it and see what it needs to feel connected again. When we are overcome by anger, we are very much in a state of separation. We might feel competitive, threatened, frustrated, or insecure. How can we come back to our true nature?

Fear has only two causes: the thought of losing what you have or the thought of not getting what you want.

B Y R O N   K A T I E

Do Not Worry

When the quick pulse of worry is racing through you like a steam train, your first impulse is probably to try to stop the train. But despite your insistence, it won't stop. An inner battle starts to unravel and it's clear you're not winning. So, honey, breathe. And get off the train. You don't have to stop it, just jump off the back.

I know one thing for sure: you are not the train. You are the beautiful, expansive countryside it's running through.

Disconnect to Reconnect

We live in a very amazing time of digital connection, yet we are overstimulated and plugged into everyone else's worries. We haven't evolved fast enough to keep up with our technological advances. A little scroll through Facebook might reveal an intense upset in the world news, a friend's scary spider invasion, a spot of political madness and someone else's problem of the day – all within a second. It might be time to unplug a bit. Have a breather and reconnect inwards. When we occupy ourselves completely, we can be brave enough to listen to our worries, the way a friend would listen to us and offer support. We might be mindful enough to notice where our energy is pulled to in those moments of scrolling and decide not to ingest stimuli that make us feel unwell.

I treat so many people for anxiety. They almost always say they feel disconnected from themselves – fragmented. If you're one of these lovely, warm, smiling people walking around with a knot in your solar plexus the size of Texas, I really want you to know you're not alone. Let's get relaxed, creative and connected...

Going Inward

First, I invite you to dive deep into this body of yours; so cleverly, so loyally and without judgement, it's feeling your feelings by translating your thoughts into emotions. Feel into your solar plexus; find it under the heart where the rib cage comes together, just under your breastbone where the softness begins at the top of the abdomen. This is the energy centre that tightens the most when we're under stress. The neighbouring heart will put up walls. It gets a message that it's time to build a fortress. The thing is, this protective measure is going to keep us away from the solution: connecting to each other and allowing the world to come in. We are at our most vulnerable and that's our greatest beauty. We want to keep our heart open to allow this energy to move through us, rather than cage it all in.

The body unquestionably listens to whatever the mind is telling it. In the grips of anxiety, it believes that danger is afoot; it sets off all your alarm bells and tightens up your diaphragm – the gateway to deep breaths and calmer feelings. So, let's start there: take a big deep breath. Place your hands on your belly, feeling the expansion of your breath into the deepest part of your lungs. Allow your rib cage to expand slightly as you do this. Let your chest open and shoulders roll back. Now push out your belly the way you did when you were a child, looking in the mirror to see how big you could make it. Feel how this simple posture is dropping your lungs down into a more spacious place, opening to take in more air. This will give you a clearer mind in just a few moments. Breathe like your belly is a balloon deflating and expanding for a few minutes. Allow your mind to come home to your body. Each breath grounding your mental awareness and discharging the momentum it was building as you nourish your nervous system with more oxygen. Your focus will shift down from your head into your hara. In Reiki we call this deep belly breathing method *Jōshin Kokyū Hō*, which means to purify the mind with the breath. As you do this, feel your mind open and expand into a spacious awareness as it harmonises with the light energy in the body.

Connecting to the life-force that is stable in your body, no matter what is going on around you, is a quick portal back to the present moment. Let's move all of your attention into the stability of your body. Feel the tingling sensation in the bottom of your feet. Notice the subtle vibrations in your hands. Follow the breath all the way to the bottom of your lungs and all the way back out, feeling that soft little breeze in your nostrils. Tune in to your pulse. There is a whole universe of activity happening right here in your body and it operates so beautifully without any need for control. Life is just like this genius body of yours. When we step out of our mind, all of this intelligent beauty becomes available to enjoy.

I invite you now to look up and notice what's around you. Try not to think as you do this, just move your eyes through the space and take in all the colours, shapes, textures. If you can see any part of nature – even just a houseplant – spend a few minutes gazing at it while keeping a little attention in your body. If you really tune into the life-force in that plant, you might begin to feel a resonance with it. You are part of nature. Your body is a gateway to connect with the physical world in a calming, refreshing and energising way.

Now that we are our calm, truer selves again, I invite you to meet your worry next time it arises with a simple question: are you truth or are you fantasy? You might discover that your anxious mind is in the future, obsessively constructing rich and unhelpful scenarios. If this is the case, just come back to the present moment and know that this is a sign of your incredible creativity. Let it go the way you would release a bad dream – because that's all it was. It doesn't have any basis in reality.

After my son was born, I experienced a level of anxiety I hadn't known was possible before. My Mama Bear protective instincts were fierce, active, loud and often based in total fiction. Once I understood the reason, it seemed to ease. And then it morphed.

I later projected anxiety towards my husband (my father's kidneys failed when I was sixteen; I didn't put two and two together at the time but having a child of my own ignited unresolved childhood fears). I noticed one night, as he read a story to our son, that my heart was racing along with my imagination. Nothing was happening – except what would have been a totally sweet and fleeting moment I could have been cherishing – but I was in my head putting plans in place for what I would do if something horrible transpired. Thankfully, a wiser, soulful awareness took over me. I realised something. What if I was right? Could I prevent that with my worry? Life always reminds me that, as it turns out, I can't control much. This put me into a softer state of surrender. If you knew this was your last day, you would want to savour it all, right? I wouldn't want to waste my last day with my love worrying about tomorrow. This shook me awake. I came to the moment. I finally arrived home with my little family, reading stories on my child's floor, noticing the beauty of his chubby little hands holding his soft little toes. I was simply sitting and listening to their sweet voices in the present moment, no longer making my own stories up in my head. If those thoughts were just manifested fear, then I feel better letting them go. If they are a premonition of some kind, fine, I'll be present for the gift of being together for this precious time. Either way this moment is as it is and I can be here, savouring the perfection of it. Anxiety is never happening because we're present; it's a story of a time that isn't real.

> The only power we have is to be fully
> here in the present, soaking in all the
> wonderful offerings of life.

There are so many details that we miss when we're in our heads. These moments of presence don't have to be saved for only special occasions; they can be used to immerse in simple pleasures. Looking at a tree while we breathe, feeling a soft connection to nature. Listening to birds celebrating the new day with their song. We can celebrate too – just for being alive in this moment, with all of its vivid details. No regrets, no worries, just happy to be here, now.

We can't drive that train or put the brakes on it, but we can get off and have a party. And we might even notice, after a short while enjoying the flowering countryside, that the train has passed. We can't even see it. And it's left behind a quietly marvellous place to explore.

Be Grateful

Gratitude is the central principle because it unlocks the very centre of ourselves: the heart. Gratitude is medicine. It takes us out of the habitual mental pattern of complaining and craving, and lands us into the very abundant now. Gratitude has been found to increase longevity, decrease depression and spark compassion. So simple, and free for all to practise in any moment. Gratitude naturally arises when we notice the splendour of life all around us. It connects us to love as we embrace the moment with our open heart.

Deep Appreciation

I notice, in perfect stillness, that gratitude is effortless. An abundant flow of deep appreciation for this moment, for life, for the miracle of existence pours from our true nature. Mindfulness is gratitude in motion. Imagine the delight of being a match struck in pure presence, whose flame is witnessed from coming to going, not just as a tool to light a fire but as a complete miracle in itself. I look around and see one miracle after another; there is so much to savour, so much to take in and appreciate. I do nothing to create or deserve this moment. All I do to unlock its riches is simply notice. That is our true state; it's what comes naturally to us when we are at peace with the world.

There is a divine miracle present within you every moment of every day. Most of the time it goes unnoticed, but it has been a vibrant source of life-force since you were only the size of a poppy seed in your mother's womb. Your heart has been beating for you long before your birth. Its steady drum doesn't ask for recognition. It doesn't judge how you use the life it provides for you. It just steadily beats a rhythmic song of gratefulness. This is a portal to the miracle of life. Your connection to the entire cosmos, the home of your soul. Your heartbeat is an ancient ritual drumming circle, the pulse of life itself, an access point to hear your soul's deepest truth and highest callings. Tune in to this sacred force. It will guide you home. It will look around with eyes of wonder to take in the miracle of existence – all made available in this very moment. If you look deeply, you might discover that everything you want is already here.

Going Inward

In Reiki we have a meditation that's very simple called Gassho (meaning putting the palms together). With our hands together, just in front of our heart, we anchor ourselves deeply into our being. We can't do anything but rest here. By placing all of our attention in our palms, we feel an energy moving there. We notice there is a tiny space between the palms. This little gap is echoed in the mind; we can take a sacred pause to refresh ourselves, feeling a gap in thoughts. With your hands like this, close your eyes and focus on something that fills you with joy. It can be anything at all, as long as it lights you up. Feeling grateful, let that emotion be amplified in your heart and reverberate out to your whole body. Then out even further into your energy field. Rest in a state of being content with the world.

Be content with what you have; rejoice
in the way things are. When you realise
there is nothing lacking, the whole world
belongs to you.

L A O   T Z U

Be True to Your Way and Your Being

Be devoted to the way of your soul. Be faithful to your true essence.

Everything about the Reiki practice is provided as a signpost to get to our truth. The True Self (your being) acting from its true nature (your way). When we are present, we are free of anger and worry, and we are grateful. We live out our true nature, which is kindness. We stop arguing with the way things are. We live in harmony. We see life with our right mind.

Our way is malleable; it changes. Sometimes your way might be brushing your teeth. It might be taking your child to school. It might be your work, or the dishes. The way is life as it's lived. When we are true to it, we approach life without a story. The mind's distortions don't tarnish how it's supposed to be, so it's allowed to be how it is. How could life be anything other than how it is?

> Being true to your being means you listen
> to that quiet voice within your heart,
> honouring the inner whispers.

As a devotee to this wise energy, it guides you to your highest path – your way. To follow the inner wisdom that is generated from your own heart will bring happiness; to go against it will create suffering. This invites us to be dedicated to our life, to give it our full attention. To be faithful to it as our loyal friend. What does this principle bring you an awareness of?

When we live from our true essence, we open to the love that we are and always have been. We arrive to the present, mind and body aligned with soul, and feel the power of that inexhaustible light within ourselves. We see life with the clarity of a mind at peace and realise our purity as portals to crystalline consciousness.

Going Inward

This particular principle tends to be one that resonates deeply with women who have been living their lives on behalf of others. It can bring up quite a lot. Our heart has been through a growth spurt, showing us where we've left it, where we were untrue to it. This opens a new level of healing. As we emerge to a new way for ourselves, we serve the being. We see that in the past it gave us red flags we simply brushed aside, and we vow to no longer ignore its tender pulse of wisdom. We will listen. We are true to it. For this one, I invite you to grab your journal and write at the top of your page: 'How am I not true to myself?' And let your heart just express all of its tender truth. Let this be an excavation of all your true feelings. Then, write on the top of a fresh page: 'How would it feel to live my truth?' And let your soul show you what life might do.

I have found that my truth is always generous.
Feel into how living aligned with your soul might
be the best for everyone.

Be Kind to Yourself and Others

Be kind. The summit of the Reiki principles and the highest expression of ourselves in the world. Kindness is love manifesting on behalf of itself. Acting it out is good for our health; it floods the body with oxytocin, inspires meaningful connection and creates positive memories. This principle is lived out in Oneness, beyond fear which stems from separation; kindness connects all beings. It tells me that your wellbeing is my own. You are my world, you live in my mind, we rest in each other. As we heal through the many layers of personal wounding by offering a little compassion to ourselves, we naturally become more compassionate to other people's pain. And then this ripple effect expands and expands. We make the whole world kinder simply by being kind one little encounter at a time.

A lot of us are experts at shortchanging ourselves. We tend to build our lives around rather limited beliefs about what we can have, or be, or do. These limited beliefs are so baseline, we don't even know that we are holding ourselves back until a truly expansive idea flies into our consideration and we notice the contrast. When we act in kindness, we give ourselves permission, and this allows others to do the same.

Going Inward

Repeating 'be kind to yourself and others' using the active meditation technique we used before, what images arise? Sometimes this one can show us where we haven't been kind. Try to stay with the place these images are leading you rather than go into regret – where can you be kinder? To yourself? To others? What is the kindest thing you can do for yourself? This doesn't always need to be a big lavish treat (although it definitely can be!) but sometimes we are guided to simple things like eating more greens, taking a day off, or going to bed earlier. What's the kindest thing you can do for a loved one? This might be simple too, like inviting them to eat dinner with you. See what your soul wants to express in this way of kindness.

The principles are guiding lights shining truth into our mind, pointing to the action that follows. The key word throughout the instruction is *be*. When we aren't being angry, we aren't identified and acting with anger. The non-action means that anger stays with us so we can heal it; it doesn't flow into the world where it can cause more destruction. When we are being grateful there is an activity attached, even if that is purring in utter contentment. When we are being true, we are aligned with the truth of reality; we cease arguing with it and enter mindfulness. We are the sum of our actions. We are our choices animated.

Choosing kindness means we act from the space of wholeness, prioritising wellbeing.

Loving kindness is the soul's way.

It forgives, and we receive a most empowered healing in the grace of that choice. Kindness is our true nature, and it feels absolutely wonderful to live out our truth. Kindness puts us in touch with every living thing and opens us to receive kindness back many times over. When we wish to make kindness our religion, it becomes an effortless way of being in the world.

Chapter 3

Our Sacred Earth

Corona Means Crown

What happened at the beginning of the coronavirus crisis? There was a wave of fear that moved across the globe as we all focused on survival. This provoked a time of deep healing – together. How very unusual to be going through something so significant across the entire world at the same moment. This was challenging, transformative, unifying and shattered many illusions. Some ran to the market to get supplies in bulk, others ran to the hills. Our primitive brain ruled for a short time as we coped with the sudden shift. All our fears surfaced from the depths of our primitive selves. Words used most often in every written message or article were 'unprecedented' and 'uncertain'; one speaks of the past, the other of the future. Was anything ever certain? The greatest challenge for many was the inability to plan. We were suddenly forced to be present. To be home with our families, or alone with ourselves. Our sense of abundance may have shifted dramatically as business changed across the world economy. This unifying suffering brought many to their knees, while opening many hearts in the process. Most of us shifted our desire from wanting more to just wanting to keep what we had.

As we began the process of collective healing in the roots, we had a chance to become more mindful. To see who in our society was considered essential. Who, perhaps only a week ago, went unnoticed. Those souls collecting the bins, the ones running the shops, delivering packages, driving the trucks, supplying food, courageously working in hospitals. We all have our roles to play, our contribution to the collective. We are each a pulse in this living organism called humanity. A breath on this larger being known as the Earth. This was a time to see who supports our lives. This was a time to reassess how busy we had been. How much we took for granted, how much we actually needed and what the environment would do if we all hit pause for several weeks. People connected to each other more. They took pleasure in nature again. Families got back in touch. Friends reached out. We could feel true empathy for what another was experiencing. The Earth was healing. The air was fresh, the stars came out, the birds wanted to sing all day. This is the root. Everything messy about being human and the essential aspect to incarnate on this world. It felt like we were all thrown down to the ground, so we could begin the process of healing from the bottom up. We were given a chance to awaken. Together. We were in the cocoon. The furnace of alchemy. Unbeknown to us, this is what we had been practising for all along.

Deep Connection

Sometimes we forget – for epochs – that we are all connected. And we need something to wake us up. Collectively we can see that now. This virus affects our respiratory system; the lungs are the wings of the heart. Here we awaken our connection and are called to listen to our soul. We are in the great pause.

Listen. Return to love. Reassess.

Our medicine is always tuning in to the Earth. To ground into the present moment, sweetly alive with her, connected to her wisdom, moving down out of our mind and deep into our body, rooted into the planet. When I connect to her, I feel her healing so forcefully underway, she makes it so. She gave us pause to clear our collective breath. We lost our old way overnight. Not just schedules, plans and money, but that feeling of certainty – though we never really had that to begin with. Can we make friends with uncertainty? It's always been our invisible companion. We have collectively been in denial about that undesirable trait of life, because we just love to be in control. But if we look, have we ever actually been in control? Can we make friends with the nature of reality? To do so means making friends with life. As it is. Accepting that we are not in control. Amongst upheaval and change what remains as the changeless? This is our work: to find this centre. To be at peace with the present moment. To abandon our habitual need-to-know mind and sink deeply into our beingness. We can learn to love the unknown.

The pandemic affected all of society at once. Our collective root chakra (the centre of energy governing safety, family and survival as our base) took a hit while we were home, healing this very aspect of life. Our tower toppled, our structures crumbled and we were in the foundations to rebuild a better world. The way of connection, compassion, unity.

From this space of surrender, creativity sprouted – a feeling of freshness after regaining our footing. People moved out of fear to be playful, creative, and found a deeper intimacy with themselves. They made boundaries, processed feelings, openly shared emotions.

We are ascending from our depths to heal on every single level. The rise shifts perspectives again – who do we want to be in this new world? Who am I after this transformation? Will we meet a new identity as humans? We are being reborn in this process, riding this energy up towards the crown from where it came – the awakening. We will give birth to this new world together. We may find the brilliance of our essence, unclouded by the doing, striving, reaching. Grounded in the being, witnessing, listening, flowing with life as it prompts us to. Our task now is to lift into the heart, to identify with each other as one world, breathing a new life into creation from the very heart of humanity.

What are we left with when it's all stripped back? What happens when we pause and go within?

There is a Sufi proverb that says, 'When the heart weeps for what it has lost, the soul rejoices for what it has found.'

Going Inward

Questions for your journal: how can I serve from my soul? How can I open my heartland to share what is true, while feeding my soul all that it guides me towards? What is my expanded self (soul) guiding me towards?

We must be willing to let go of the life
we planned so as to have the life that is
waiting for us.

JOSEPH CAMPBELL

There Are No Desires in Oneness

The Earth doesn't 'want' for this tree to survive, for whether it grows upwards or dissolves into her, the tree *is* the Earth. She doesn't want or wish the conditions of herself to be different to what they are; she evolves in surrender, reincarnating into her shifted timelines with grace. Her drama is a creative expression; whether ice or fire, she has no preference – she is it all. She is as much the crystal as the caterpillar; she's the air and the soil, the fire and the water. She can be it all, and it's only in being it all that she can know herself in such dynamic possibility. Her existence is temporary, evolving with each revolution. She is one with her whole self. She does not judge her expressions of life – she is life. In its fullness, in its richness. She moves, she turns, she stretches, shifts, births entirely new species as she swallows others into her past.

She does not cling to what she has been,
for she is always moving forward into
what is becoming. She is consciousness
as pure being – our wise and wild
teacher.

She is the container for life, receiving the solar seeds to water and explore.

What she has made is uniquely hers. And while we must assume there are other planets flourishing with life in other corners of this infinitely vast Universe, we can surmise that there are not any worlds exactly like her. None that have evolved as she has. Just like there can't be another soul out there that has had the life you have had, made the decisions you've made and reached the place you are now. We know our time with her is precious – as souls and as a species that's sprouted from her fertile ground. To know her is to love her.

We are the cells in the body of this planet. We don't look to our own cells in our physical bodies with any desire for a particular one to survive; we see them as elements of ourselves in flux, supporting our being as they come and go, adapt, change, flow. This is how she sees us.

We are part of her, we as she. She as we.

Sit on the Earth

Sit on the Earth
Be still
Feel her move
Sensing how she carries you
Through infinite space.

Lie beneath an ancient tree
Looking deeply at its presence
Witness the rivers of life-force energy
Dancing.

Notice your breath
The rhythm of your heartbeat
Slip beneath the choppy waves of the mind
Into the deep bliss of pure being
And lose your edges
Resting in that delicious blending with All That Is
(Which is all that is you).

Look at the sky above
Witness clouds fade and return
On the endless canvas
Nothing leaves a trace.

Feel the heat
From your nearest star
It knows nothing
But offering light
Close your eyes
Accept that light
And know that it is you
You *are* that light.

The miracle is not to walk on water. The miracle is to walk on earth.

LINJI YIXUAN

She Speaks

The space between you and me is an illusion. That perceived distance is full of little atoms dancing at different speeds. We are just clumps of particles quivering with elation in form. In all those atoms there is space, and in all that space there is energy.

We are pure energy. When we connect to the Earth, we connect to her energy field, her fertility, her ripeness, her abundance. Her timeline. Today as she held me, she whispered. I sank deeply into her maternal embrace. The space in our atoms merged into one.

I am in no rush to be anything,
I just am.

I cycle through seasons,
through Ages,
through Aeons.

I move eternally around the sun
while he moves around the galaxy,
while she is reaching into the Universe,
all while space itself expands.

Nothing is still. And we leave no trace as we journey deeper into this expansive cosmos.

We are moving as one. Heartbeats. Lava flows. Tigers and mountains.

Slow down. Feel the consonance of my pulse. Feel life. It is all happening right here. Right now.

The slower you go, the higher you vibrate. Synch into my current and I will hold you as I always have. I am your first mother.

Before concepts divided me into 'tree' and 'river' and 'sky,' I just was.

You've named us Earth, Moon, Sun – yet we are the Universe. We have no name.

Life, Universe, Earth. Source. Pure consciousness. Knowing itself. Playing with extremes, dancing through cycles, moving through a scale of infinite frequency.

Before you call memories 'yesterday' and dreams 'future', you just are. Always in the ever-unfolding moment of now. You are you. On me. Of me. As me. An extension of me.

You say you're 'these many years old' as if you possess that age – as if it was *yours*. That is just how many times I've circled a star since your birth. How can a deathless energy be born?

You, me, this, that – all pretend. Just names. Disguises.

We Are the Earth

As I lie upon her, hugging her, she holds me in an enveloping embrace. I offer her Reiki as an act of love, as a means of connection; she soon breathes me in. I feel her fertility echoed in my womb. I feel her creativity, her sensuality, her strength. She contains my entire existence in just this moment. There is no record of where I began to her because she feels me as herself. There is as much of a trace of me as there is of the bird moving across the sky. I melt into her pulse. Her life-force vibrates through me.

My energy swirls as it greets hers – womb to womb. She receives me. I am for a moment becoming as vast as She, connected to it all. I feel my sense of self travel through a vacuum; the loss of this ghostly self is at once delicious and terrifying. To realise what is happening causes me to re-identify as me again, and out of the vacuum I come, back to the world of illusions. Back to separation lying here on this sand as a woman nestled onto the beach. Sand, sea, sky, woman – naming them defines them as separate entities.

We are fragmented. A mind in pieces looking at itself from every possible angle, searching for the essence from which it came.

Yet we are love and anything we feel as less is our innocent craving for what we are. There is only love and that which seeks to be loved.

The Sea

My mother's family comes from Crete. While visiting my grandmother there, I rediscovered my love for the Mediterranean. For the sea.

Dipping into those crystalline waters, something pure and ancient stirred as I swam through the soft pinks towards the horizon, silky saltwater reflecting every hue of the setting sun. Violet, gold, rose. I easily slip into that perfect state of no-thought. I began to hear whispers. Verses that activate wise, inner wisdom – bringing it from the background to the front of our awareness.

Something happens to me when I swim in these ancestral waters. Actually, when I float. In a state of surrender, something deep within me rises. Memories bubble up. A quiet confidence washes over me. Amongst that flowing movement, profound stillness.

Going Inward

Say it with me as if we are floating on sacred waters together: I am ready to trust. I am ready to be carried towards my soul's greatest calling. I am ready for my beckoning heart to be fulfilled. I'm willing to release the struggle and surrender to life's ocean of energy.

That water whispers to me. We must connect to our bodies, to our Earth. She holds us so effortlessly. She is our home to nurture as she has nurtured us. We are her. We are nature. We are all the abundant celebration for the life that she is.

The Silent Sermon

The moon is just behind my shoulder as the sun rises in front of me. I have been left with a sensation of fullness because I found something empty – a hole to wholeness.

I hadn't expected to find her. I was simply exploring the coastline near our little holiday home, wandering the Portuguese cliffs with curiosity. Carved by nature in a jagged orange rock was a near perfect circle framing the sea beyond like a portal. I walked around the edge to peer through, finding a full female form sculpted by the sea into the red rock, a circle on top of a triangle like an archaic symbol of the female form, revealing a space that so moved me I stood transfixed in absolute reverence. It's simply an elegant round space with waves coming and going, but standing in complete awe, I watch the Earth receive herself. She is the Goddess embodied. This beautiful, hidden-away pocket of nature where land meets water is reflecting to me what has been softly silencing my mind.

> We are containers of light receiving the light that we are. We are love holding space for love.

We live in shapes that elude to a separate form – a boundary of skin – yet we are merely energy, consciousness awakening to consciousness. Experiencing concepts of a self wash away is the most beautiful realisation we can aspire to understand. Self-realisation is the realisation that there is no self. This loss provides us with everything. Spaciousness is our essence.

She whispers without words, offering a silent sermon for the way things truly are. She sang a song to invite us to merge there in that love that bonds without attachment. To lose ourselves so we may know ourselves. At once we die and are reborn to the vast self – the one that contains all.

She has reminded me that this is who I am.

Whole and peaceful.
Empty.
Open.

When we are worried, angry, or depressed, it is this version of ourselves we long for – this one that holds it all and yet holds nothing at all. We return home by releasing whatever is causing us pain. We can change our mind and align in this still point at the shore, letting waves of endless joy lap eternally at our heart.

God spoke today in flowers, and I, who
was waiting on words, almost missed the
conversation.

INGRID GOFF-MAIDOFF

The Medium Between
My Soul and Life

I am grateful for my hands. There is magic flowing through them.

My feet take me everywhere I wish to go. They give me the sweet experience of movement upon this miracle of a planet.

I am grateful for my heart. It beats in harmony with the heart of the Universe. I listen with my ears just below the surface while submerging my thoughts in the still water of the bathtub. It bellows in a rhythmic chant that tranquillises mental noise and calls me home.

I love the skin that contains me, that gives me a sense of the air around me, that speaks to me with its sensory intelligence. I feel the world with it, and I am felt. It grants me the illusion of separation so I can know myself as this version of me, as this avatar.

I cherish these eyes that see the world in rich colours and tidy compositions. I marvel at the delights in sound that my ears can host.

I look in the mirror at a body that has always adored me. I

breathe into the safety of this body, the harbour for my mind to rest.

Despite constant criticism, you have just loved me; you have given me the generous gift of a space to live through. I'm so very blessed to have you. You are my personal, delicious, sensuous experience of life itself. Body of mine, you are the medium between my soul and this Earth. I vow to treat you well – in my dialogue, in my thoughts, in my ways of nurturing you and decorating your curvy form. I love being with you. You are my safety net when my mind wanders off to a future imagining. You are always here for me to come home to. As soon as I arrive, I notice that you are always warm for me. You are beautiful. I smile at you. I love you. Thank you.

Going Inward

Place a hand on your heart, and the other on your hara, and come to your inner stillness:

Breathing in,
I recognise the presence of my body.
Breathing out,
I smile to my body.
Breathing in,
I recognise the Earth within my body.
Breathing out,
I smile to the Earth.
Breathing in,
I recognise the element of water within my body.
Breathing out,
I smile to the water.

Breathing in,
I recognise the element of fire within my body.
Breathing out,
I smile to the fire.
Breathing in,
I recognise the air within my body.
Breathing out,
I smile to the air.
Breathing in,
I recognise spaciousness within my body.
Breathing out,
I smile to space.
Breathing in,
I recognise consciousness within my body.
Breathing out,
I smile to consciousness.
Breathing in,
I recognise my ancestors alive in my body.
Breathing out,
I smile at my ancestors.
Breathing in,
I recognise life within my body.
Breathing out,
I smile at life.
Breathing in,
I recognise the Universe within my body.
Breathing out,
I smile to the Universe.

The Care and Feeding
of a Light-Bringer

As you weave your web of light, you shift the tides among human beings from fear to love. From violence to kindness. This is what you were born for. This is why you're here. For an open-hearted soul like you, times like these can be daunting. It's vital to look after yourself, to stay connected to yourself, to reach out for support when you need it and to be as optimistic as you can. When we are busy supporting others, it can be easy to forget about ourselves. But if we prioritise our own wellbeing, we find that serving others comes easy.

Your web pulsates with increasing luminosity when you look after yourself most of all.

What Lights You Up? What Nourishes Your Soul?

Is it nature? That reliable wonder opens your heart. It anchors your soul. Is it birdsong, listened to with a still mind? Is it the sunshine, creating artwork, or swimming in the sea? Maybe it's writing gratitude lists under the sacred light of the moon. Investigate and make these things part of your routine energy maintenance. Carve out time for you to do whatever it is that keeps you bright, as ritual that nourishes you from the inside out. Grab your journal and list ten nourishments.

What Food Makes Your Body Feel Like It's Glowing?

Greens, proteins, grains? Notice what you feed yourself and how it makes you feel. Understand the impact on the environment and bring consciousness to what you choose to ingest. Rather than make hard and fast rules that feel restrictive, try quietly experimenting with eating only what makes you feel energised. This will look different for everyone. Listen to what your intuition is telling you and what your body is communicating. Honour what this dear, precious vessel is asking for.

How Can You Listen to Your Soul?

It speaks to you with downloads of love. It is here to experience itself and to light up in love. So, nurture your mind with acts of kindness and practise gratitude. Consume healthy media. Our energy does not benefit from devouring large screens of panic. Be very mindful of what you put in front of your eyes. They consume whatever you place before them very quickly. See fear-based thoughts for what they are: a request for healing.

Does Your Environment Light You Up?

Create a beautiful environment for yourself to occupy. With body, home and people. Reflect your soul into these spaces to mirror your essence and bring you back to light when you're most in need. Amplify your uniqueness. Surround yourself with a community of light-bringers. Let them echo your soul's truth to you when you most need to hear it. Sit in circle with each other as often as you can.

Beautiful anchor for the light – thank you for your contribution here on this beautiful planet at this special time. Please don't be discouraged. We are working together to illuminate the shadows. They were always there, but not always seen. We are healing through sacred awareness. We're in this together and there is supportive energy all around us. Remember to reach out. You are never alone.

Going Inward

- Consider your physical body – what makes it feel nurtured, energised, alive?

- Consider your mind – what helps you feel clear-headed and inspired?

- Consider your spirit – how can you anchor into your heart and commune more deeply with your soul?

My personal self-care routine involves a long walk amongst tall trees, which relaxes both my body and mind while opening a creative flow. Forest bathing is so restorative. Most of this book was revealed by catching whispers as I walked through parks. A few words here and there would trickle into my quiet movements, and I'd pause to get them down before they passed me by. The whispers became the backbone of this book.

Journaling helps me feel connected and inspired; my journal is the best therapist in the world. Whenever something comes up, I take it to the page and let my higher self come through to sort through my confusion. It always helps.

Spending time doing something creative, following the gentle nudges of my soul, makes my spirit feel cherished. Sometimes it's very small things like changing the way my altar looks, dancing with my son, exploring a new place, or playing a singing bowl. Any activity we view as playful can have very profound benefits to our mental health.

When I carve this time into my schedule and safeguard my self-care, I notice how much better I serve my clients. I'm a happier mum who's able to enjoy the present moment and I'm a better partner to my husband too. It's so basic, yet surprisingly it can go out the window so easily. If you're reading this, then you likely care for others before yourself; we are far more able to serve when we've made looking after ourselves a priority.

Plants need water, light, nutritious soil and a little space in order to flourish – and so do you.

You Have Arrived

In deeply loving the way things are, we deeply love the way that we are. And with no resistance, no struggle to make anything into anything it isn't, we are free. We accept the Earth and all who walk upon it as sisters and brothers, beings to honour in a shared experience of divinity. Nothing is more sacred than the present moment. Nowhere is more precious than the here and now. This is the only long-lasting way to be peaceful. We give life our full attention; we let time be the great alchemist that it always has been, while we revere all that we encounter as a means of loving the inner Buddha. This inner awakened being is quietly witnessing, perpetually inside of us, healing with its compassionate presence. Because nothing belongs to it, it holds the entire world.

I walk around the bend in the park and come upon an orchestra. Leaves quivering in the wind, a far-off stream of cars, belly laughter dancing over the hill, the song voices make as they inaudibly converse, and a creaky fence bangs shut creating percussion. As I listen intently to this symphony, my mind is perfectly still and receptive. The ungraspable essence of life rises to greet me. Pain becomes a mere sensation and softens in my body. Life seems more alive – yet all that shifted was my awareness. Presence arrived and became one with the moment, while I joined with the miraculousness of ordinary life. This, by far, is the most glorious place to live. Arriving to an orchestra that doesn't wait to be heard. No desire to be anywhere else – no future, no past. You are already where you want to be. Your happy place is right here, right now, as this miraculous being. You are the shining light of consciousness, becoming more and more radiant with the simplicity of your complete presence. You have arrived. Welcome home.

Chapter 4

A Return to
Wholeness

Heal

Heal

/hēl/

Verb.

To make sound or whole.

The Two That Are One

There is this ancient undiluted energy of you, simultaneously existing within the framework of the fragmented primitive self. The soul and the personality. We are both, seeing through twin lenses concurrently – alive in a world of duality. We incarnate in this world as two things: a formless being in human form. Our seeking for unity between these two parts is an inner compulsion that manifests in an outward expression. A microcosm of the macro. Because 'as above, so below', the union of our split being inspires those around us to harmonise their two selves. And it goes on and on.

And only in this place of complete acceptance, of absolutely welcoming these two aspects of self to co-exist, can we wish to harmonise the polarity of the outer world. We collectively long for wholeness within ourselves and want nothing more than to see this wholeness reflected through our species, our world.

Healing encapsulates all of it. The journey to wholeness is heroic; we face our fears, our pain, we do a Marie Kondo and get all the skeletons out of the closet so we can see how much we've accumulated. Wrapped up in the process is the beauty and courage of our humanity. Through healing we awaken; through awakening, we heal.

The Vibration of Presence

In the same year that I experienced some of the more heart-clenching challenges I've ever faced, I became a mother and opened a Reiki practice. It was an organic transition out of my photography career. As clients started to come for Reiki, clients started to drop from photography. Within eighteen months, one line of work had replaced the other with such subtlety, I never had a last day or any marker to celebrate the full transition's completion. That's really the nature of Reiki; it can be a force that barges in and clears the decks of all the things that aren't serving us (I've definitely been on the receiving end of that), but sometimes, it's just softly filling our lives up with this fresh water while the stale washes out.

My son's birth marked a significant rebirth for me. I began my quest to find the light within and it began to awaken. After a miscarriage, shortly followed by very different yet exceptionally pivotal trips to India and Iceland, I had a spontaneous kundalini awakening one afternoon in our East End London garden. It was coincidentally the date that I would have been due had that first pregnancy been successful. I had been meditating and then what felt like a bolt of lightning struck me from crown to root. I vibrated. I shook. I sizzled. It was the most incredible, electrifying experience. I lay on the Earth hugging her for over an hour to ground what was happening, and later that day I became pregnant again.

With a foot in both worlds, I started reaching into what it would be like to focus on spiritual work as my work, developing my intuition so I could facilitate a connection for others to the love that is on the other side (I now prefer to connect them to the love that is inside). To back up a bit... Six years before this electric awakening my father had passed away. He'd spent eleven long years on dialysis and within that time had two failed attempts to have a kidney transplant. He was fifty-five when he left his body. I went to visit him and my family in Virginia two months before it happened. I could sense that he was leaving the physical realm. He appeared to do so consciously, because I could see his essence beginning to pull away. It was clear that he was mentally preparing; all our conversations were retrospective. When it was time to return to London, I hugged him goodbye and as I walked down the stairs towards the front door, I felt like an invisible leash was around my neck tugging me back up to hug him one last time. Back in London, I immediately scheduled time off from my job and booked another flight home to have those last moments with him.

I missed him by ten days.

It was a very surreal time, yet his departure from the manifest world was by far the greatest leap in my spiritual development. I didn't understand the physics of it, but I was still aware of his presence. I knew when he was in the room and when he had ventured further afield. Dad's shift to the other side had taken my awareness into that space with him. At first it was a sensation, a feeling, a knowing. It was very subtle. He didn't assert himself. I just knew he was there, and I could sense where he was standing, and then I'd feel a shift of energy when he left. This led me to actively developing my intuitive ability so I could help others do the same. It was quite a long and winding journey from my first Reiki attunements in 2004, to finding this latent mediumship in 2008, to realising the best possible medicine didn't need to come from outside of ourselves in 2015 when my son was born. My understanding of healing the void that grief can carve had shifted – from filling it in with our loved one's presence, to filling it in with our own presence.

I saw several clients who took their longing for approval from physical people into the spiritual world – and then the seeking was still disempowering them as they looked to a non-physical entity to provide the answers. After having been there myself and seeing this echo in my consultations, I decided to focus solely on healing – supporting people to find their own inner authority in their soul, empowered as a whole, integrated being.

I've been privileged to witness clients embark on this pilgrimage to wholeness as they move towards the energy of who they really are. Seeing their spiralling pathways fills me with complete awe. To see this homeward journey is always a fresh experience, as if it's perpetually the very first one anyone's ever stepped out upon.

The nature of energy medicine is that it gives us exactly what we need; it meets us where we are. So, if we need physical or emotional healing, that's what we'll receive. If we need guidance, we'll get it directly from our own source of wisdom, our inner spiritual counsel – the part of us that already knows. This source is always available for beloved support within our intuition; it's found just on the other side of our busy mind.

We have all the answers already. We don't need anything outside of ourselves to give us validation – whether a physical person or advanced non-physical being.

Deep within us the entire Universe pulses
as us.

It is in the sweet, vast inner sanctuary of our heart that we meet our soul and ultimately find what we all crave – experiencing the spectacular brightness of the True Self. It is here that we no longer feel separate or in need of anything external to bring us joy. We realise that our essence is love expressed as joy. Everyone has the ability to heal oneself, some just need the space for this knowing to rise.

I don't call myself a healer. That's just not a very accurate title. I am not doing the healing, just holding a present, welcomed space for healing to happen.

Presence is healing to receive.

Our alignment with the inner being opens us to all the wisdom and power of the cosmos. When we return to our body with one conscious breath, our body relaxes and healing is automatic. Another holding us in the energy of presence can allow us to receive an attunement to the blissful frequency of our own soul. This is what holding space means. It's a well-known aspect of alchemy; transformation can only happen within a container. So, by coming into the deepest place within ourselves and connecting to another's deepest dimension, we create this beautiful open space that serves as the container for them to meet themselves. The vibration of presence is fluid, intelligent and self-perpetuating. It creates a bridge to the soul, which invites both minds into this sphere of healing. The healing happens on its own as we surrender to the infinite spaciousness of peace.

We bow in service to the soul. We seek to guide others home to their inner sanctuary, offering a space for soul communion – an invitation to meet the whole, awakened self. This is what I wish to happen in and amongst these pages – an extension of those sessions, where you can meet you and rest within the luminous temple of your inner heart. You are a completely empowered being who is deserving of healing, joy and fulfilment. It is your birthright. Your divine inheritance. The way of things.

Peace is available to you in every moment.

Joy is here for you in every moment.

Freedom is possible in every moment.

You dissolve discord, heal pain, dispel unconsciousness — without doing anything — simply by being and holding that frequency of intense presence.

ECKHART TOLLE

The Body as a Map

Healing is our nature. Connection is our truth. When we come back to wholeness in our mind and heart, our body blissfully follows. Awakening is a medicine of congruence; it is holistic by its very nature, bringing us back into full alignment with our whole self while working across our whole life.

> The soul lives in timeless awareness, and while the mind is an expert time-traveller, the body is always present.

Your body carries with it a map of all its unprocessed emotional pain, loyally storing a wealth of information we can easily uncover. My clients are always fascinated that I can pinpoint what's going on in their lives just by listening to them say where the pain is in the body. A lovely woman came to see me with swelling in her left cheek and pain in her left jaw, which was causing irritation in her left ear. Knowing the keys to the treasure map, I asked her if she was having any difficulty communicating with her mother. This revelation was met with wide, surprised eyes; a look from someone who is being understood by a stranger is precious to witness. Of course, the answer was yes. Rather than using any psychic means of discovery, I had simply translated her body's dialect to a message that helped her to see what needed healing in her life. The real cause of a physical issue is almost always an emotional one. Although we tend to view our body and our emotions as two distinct phenomena, the body *is* emotion.

The body is an elaborate messenger, telling us where in our life we need to cultivate healing. Once you uncover these codes, you can understand the source of pain and work to heal the cause rather than the effect. That is the meaning of holistic; we try to understand the whole picture, so we treat the root cause rather than just the symptoms. If someone is experiencing a heart condition, breathing difficulties and pain in their mid-back, a holistic health practitioner will help them to see this is all happening around their heart chakra. What are the deeper issues that need healing in this person's life? Are they having challenges with their relationships? Are they able to acknowledge their emotions? We'll dive into the chakras next.

The Hero's Journey

Imagine as a soul we descend from the non-physical formless realm of universal consciousness into the physical realm of form. We find ourselves alive within the dualism of planet Earth, having gone through the journey of manifestation while forgetting our origin as spiritual beings. As we travel down the chakras to root into the manifested world, the layers get denser and denser – from consciousness to light to sound to air to fire to water to earth. The frequencies slow down, from something vibrating too fast to be seen in the 3D world, to a slow, long cycle – very much manifest with all the senses of a physical body. Each chakra corresponds to a wavelength and a dimension of reality. Relating to the body and to the non-physical experience, our energy centres share properties in the metaphysical as well as the physical.

At the root, we are made manifest in a body, we touch the Earth with our feet, legs and the base of our spine. This lower realm is occupied with our most base needs in a physical reality – our survival as a human being, as out of touch with the idea of our eternal nature as could possibly be. This is the chakra of separation – of being in a body as an individual, with a life that is constantly in need of maintenance and protection. To be strong enough to survive, we need a community – a group of people we can root ourselves in with. We need a shelter to base ourselves and nourishment.

If any of these are threatened, our fear kicks in, perhaps even anger if the threat comes from another human being. When we are grounded into the Earth and have a feeling of general stability in our life, we have a strong base upon which to build our sacred emotional and creative experience. If this base chakra is not healthy, anything we create on top of it will be unstable. This correlates to family, home, physical vitality, work and money. The heavier emotions which are based on the concepts associated with this chakra are also likely to become buried here – primarily grief, anger and fear. When in balance we can operate in this world as part of it, we experience health and know the limitless nature of Earth's abundance. We experience a stability within our life that feels deeper than the conditions of living in a world of unstable forms. Grounding activities are often neglected in our modern age, as we, as a species, have evolved from our primitive days of the root chakra to the adolescent age of the solar plexus. Rather than rest and nourish, we take pride in busyness and pushing forward. We have ascended into the ego's habitat, the narrowly focused mental arena, and our task as a collective is to continue into the spacious heart for the next phase of our evolution. The chakras are an upward journey into enlightenment, each having a chapter to experience in the hero's journey home. We can't skip through the chapters to the end as each forms a continuum where our understanding is cumulative.

The Chakras as Evolutionary Journey

As babies, we were only concerned with our survival; we were completely dependent on our parents to provide that for us. We used our only tool to make sure we lived: our voice. We'd cry to make sure our needs were met. Babies are souls manifesting as human, completely enmeshed in the experience of the root chakra. As we grow to toddlers, we begin to feel our emotions, to play and to get creative. The phase of the sacral experience is consumed with how we relate to others and our world. As teenagers we go through the awkward transition of puberty, and our solar plexus. We live for our independence; we strive to find out who we are and what we want to do with our lives. We depart from the powerful need to be part of our family and value the feeling of friendship over all else. We become eager to belong and seek approval from our peers. We either have a lucky break with popularity and feel confident in ourselves, or we are the norm and totally insecure. We need outside validation because we lack the understanding of our heart; we are too young to realise that the world can never satisfy the insatiable desire for our own approval. This is the realm of the ego's trappings and where we find ourselves as a species. I have found that what is true on an individual level will also be true for the collective as a whole. So, as we are tasked with moving through our own journey home, so is humanity. We are still adolescents. Our role now is to move into young adulthood – to begin to feel into the expanse of the heart. This is the home of all that we have ever wanted. We don't need to fit in and find where we belong, because in this sweet and tender space we find our soul – our very essence – complete yet always evolving. From the heart we begin to feel what is true, and we know without a doubt that we are connected to it all. This is wholeness. Healing.

Realising Who You Truly Are

Imagine if our species could live from the heart as a whole; we would not see each other as threats, we would rather collaborate towards our conscious evolution, to experience our true nature while in form. We would heal how we relate to one another. From this place, we move up with all the wisdom of the heart into the throat; we express our truth. We create, we speak about what is coming up from the heart, we give it a voice and an outward vibration. This is the maturity of the forties, where we finally value our truth over how we are seen. And then as we grow older, we move into wisdom – the third eye which sees and knows, and the crown is the crone who integrates and understands. As the journey unfolds, each chakra is strengthened by the upward expansion to realise our True Self.

The chakras ascend in spiralling energy towards the direction of liberation, yet also in the descent of manifestation. Always, we have two currents of energy running up and down our energy body. In yoga this is referred to as the Shakti and the Shiva. Shiva is perpetually cascading downwards to meet Shakti, who is always unfurling upwards to meet Shiva. These are seen as the primordial energies of all of creation. The mother and the father. While Shakti is the divine aspiration of the human soul, Shiva is the irresistible attraction of divine grace. If you have a clear idea, inspiration (meaning: in spirit) comes like a flash, you envision the end result and you speak about it – begin to share the idea, talk to others to help you make sense of the path it wants to take. Then you begin to feel into it, experiencing the richness of it fully in your heart. With the solar plexus you move into action, you give it your unique energy, move it downwards still to begin creating it from the sacral, until it itself becomes a birthed form in the world with its own life-path to liberation. It's not enough to have an idea; we must give it the Earth-based practicalities of action to bring it into an Earth-based form. When it finally manifests in the world – whether a child, a creative project, or a business – it will evolve along its own path of liberation through the chakras from root to crown.

With our emotions, we want to move energy upwards to liberate ourselves. The tendency amongst us all (especially amongst the British) is to shove it all down – swallow our emotions along with our pride. They become lodged in our lower chakras – heavy weights that make us feel stuck. To release them, we need to first recognise that they are there, feel them and allow them to make us uncomfortable. Only in our willingness to see what we've hidden can we unearth and release. In our throat we either speak to a loved one, a professional, or ourselves. As Reiki practitioners, we can hold space for our emotions as they bubble up in self-treatments. We contemplate the principles. In our willingness to witness the reality of things – the truth – we can transform the feelings through tears or compassionate understanding.

Root Chakra

Location: Base of spine
Main focus: Physical existence, survival
Element: Earth
Colour: Red
Sanskrit: *Muladhara* (meaning 'root' and 'support')
Positive expressions when in balance: Stability, abundance, patience, vitality, groundedness, presence
Challenging expressions when out of balance: Lack, fear, restlessness, feeling stuck, inflexible, longing for home, anger

Physical body: Legs, knees, feet, hips, elimination system
Gland: Adrenals (this isn't the physical correlation but rather the relation of the fight/flight/freeze response)
Themes: Safety, grounding, money, home, job, vitality, family
Tools to nurture: Nature walks, the forest, gardening, eating root vegetables, walking barefoot on grass, exercise, support network, mindfulness, dance, proper rest
Affirmation: I am grounded, safe and secure. I am here. I am.

Sacral Chakra

Location: Below naval at soft part of the belly (womb space)
Main focus: Emotions, creativity
Element: Water
Colour: Orange
Sanskrit: *Svadhisthana* (meaning 'where your being is established' or 'one's own abode')
In balance: Creative flow, pleasure, sensuality, joy, adaptability, fertility
Out of balance: Overtly sexual (or not at all), trapped trauma, unsatisfying relationships, unable to relate to self or others, ungrounded, uninspired, out of touch with gut instincts
Physical body: Reproductive system, lower digestive organs, kidneys, lower back
Gland: Sexual/reproductive
Themes: Relationships, instincts, intimacy, pleasure, imagination, the unconscious
Tools to nurture: The sea, swimming, salt baths, journaling, creative expression
Affirmation: I am creative. It is safe for me to feel my feelings. I am worthy.

Solar Plexus Chakra

Location: Below breastbone
Focus: Ego, individuality, power, identity
Element: Fire
Colour: Yellow
Sanskrit: *Manipura* (meaning 'lustrous gem')
In balance: Confidence, drive, enthusiasm, leadership, solar energy, inner fire
Out of balance: Low self-esteem, narcissism, lethargy, guilt, anxiety, directionlessness
Physical body: Digestion, diaphragm, liver, stomach, spleen, small intestine, middle back
Gland: Pancreas
Themes: Individuality, identity, belonging, purpose, confidence, determination
Tools to nurture: Fire rituals, deep breathing, teamwork, courage, movement/exercise
Affirmation: I can. I act confidently in service to my soul.

Heart Chakra

Location: Centre of chest
Focus: Love, soul, connection
Element: Air
Colour: Green (and pink)
Sanskrit: *Anāhata* (meaning 'unstruck')
In balance: Love, trust, healing, compassion, connection
Out of balance: Cut off, lonely, heartbroken, lack of emotion/numbness, heaviness, dark night of the soul
Physical body: Respiratory system, immune system, physical heart, lungs, upper and middle back, arms, hands, shoulders (as gateway from heart to throat)

Gland: Thymus
Themes: Unconditional love, unity, balance, generosity, limitless, infinite, the bridge between three chakras of formless and the three chakras of form, openness
Tools to nurture: The breath, friendship, hugs, meditation, inner work, journaling, working with the hands
Affirmation: I am loving and lovable. I am love. I am connected. I am home. I am whole. It is safe for me to love and be loved. I am vast.

Throat Chakra

Location: Centre of throat
Focus: Truth, self-expression
Element: Sound
Colour: Light blue
Sanskrit: *Vishuddha* (meaning 'purification')
In balance: Clear communication, synchronicity, purpose, artistry, service, expressing the True Self
Out of balance: Not listening, speaking nervously, not able to voice truth, compare and despair, seeking approval, inability to speak up. Sore throat a common symptom.
Physical body: Voice, neck, throat, parathyroid, ears, jaw, mouth, shoulders
Gland: Thyroid
Themes: Self-expression, vibration, creativity, truth
Tools to nurture: Chanting, singing, journaling, deep listening, speaking up, reflecting
Affirmation: I am divinely guided by my deepest purpose. I know my truth and it is safe for me to speak my truth. I am true.

Third Eye Chakra

Location: Middle of brow
Focus: Insight, clarity
Element: Light
Colour: Indigo/Purple
Sanskrit: *Ajna* (meaning 'command' or 'summon')
In balance: Intuitive guidance, dreams, vision, clear perception, insight, inspiration
Out of balance: Muddied thoughts, misunderstanding, confusion, uninspired
Physical body: Eyes, ears (between throat and third eye), brain, hypothalamus, head, face
Gland: Pituitary
Themes: Imagination, spiritual awareness, consciousness, clear-seeing, clarity
Tools to nurture: Skygazing, meditation, imagination, mindfulness
Affirmation: I am light. I am guided. I see. I am clear.

Crown Chakra

Location: Top of head
Focus: Spiritual connection, compassion, wisdom, enlightenment
Element: Consciousness
Colour: Violet/White
Sanskrit: *Sahasrara* (meaning 'thousand-petalled lotus' or 'seat of God')
In balance: Wisdom, unity, awareness, understanding, compassion, bliss
Out of balance: Misunderstanding, fuzzy mind, pessimistic, unable to see bigger picture

Physical body: Brain
Gland: Pineal
Themes: Enlightenment, knowledge, self-realisation, completion, connection to All That Is, Oneness
Tools to nurture: Stargazing, meditation, kindness
Affirmation: I am one with everything. I am connected. I am peaceful. I understand.

The greatest healing would be to wake up from what we are not.

MOOJI

The Welcomed Self

Let's bow in service to love. Let's allow joy to be our guide. These are the frequencies of pure soul.

Our soul is the beautiful light of awakened consciousness, arms outstretched to welcome all, back to love. Back to itself. The soul's energy is healing by design.

When we fixate on the denser identity within our dual nature, we feel that we've lost ourselves, or disconnected from something too precious to articulate. This journey to awakening is not as grand as becoming enlightened; it's very simply recognising that we are made of two parts and finding our way back to soul alignment. Not in rejection of the ego, but compassionately integrating all parts of ourselves. That is true wholeness. When we allow, heal and truly love the whole self – not after an edit, not in a future time, but right now as we are – then nothing can ever have power over us because we are completely empowered. We scoop up all those lost parts of ourselves, kiss the forehead of each little piece and love our way back to wholeness. We can't get rid of toxic emotions; we can only accept them and love them back to health. That love alchemises the lead of our pain into the gold of our evolution. Any other way that shuns suffering or punishes ego is still a fragmented self.

Fragmented people are bound to duality. From duality sprouts polarity, opposition, self-serving behaviour and war. When we welcome ourselves – the light, dark and full gradient between – we begin to see beyond the illusion of duality while false obstacles to love dissolve. We return to love. The love we've always been.

Skeletons may haunt a person for seventy years – wounds from childhood made before one could define the experience. These are castaways that have waited for love to bring them home. Naturally, the keeper of these skeletons would just want them to go away, to leave her alone. Or to believe they need to forgive the one that put them there. But those wounded skeletons are no longer manifest as a record of the event. They only live in the mind as a memory, a trauma from losing a part of ourselves. How do we reconcile this lost pain as it lingers outside in the abyss? It doesn't happen by discarding it or minimising it by telling ourselves it's only a memory. Instead, we must look at this inner child who has hurt all these years and at last invite her to come close, to look at the version of us that is hurting – that little girl, that adolescent, the lost me from yesterday – love her, comfort her, ask her to live in the heart once more.

Going Inward

Sit with your inner child and question the beliefs that make them suffer. The inner child matures and heals in this invitation, and once they have integrated back home, they ascend. In complete presence we become one. And we are stronger for having them. At last, we are whole.

To the Healers

It takes a village to heal a world.

We need you doing your work with others, yet, the healing begins with you. If you want to live in a peaceful world, you will need to make peace in your internal world first. It starts within your own mind, your own body, your own journey. And then it happens in your home, with your family and beloveds. Outwards it goes from there to focus on your relationships and heal in all the encounters you have in your communities. Healing the world does not need to happen on a grander scale than this. It will spread beyond you like a wildfire. Lightwork is a catching thing. Imagine for a moment that millions of others like you are working to heal themselves back to a state of wholeness while beaming their light, offering an outpouring of healing to all who meet them. Each time one of you lights up, you ignite another, and on it goes. If you want to heal the world, fall in love with yourself completely, love your family, love your neighbours, learn to be an example of loving kindness to everyone you meet.

As you come home to your wholeness, you carve an easier path for the person next to you. As you work to make peace in your own mind, you are working towards a peaceful world. We cannot make peace with thoughts that war.

When you've been in the trenches with all your own pain and offered love to yourself in the most intimate space of allowing, you cultivate a deep sense of compassion for all beings. This is the medicine of our time.

Your commitment to self-healing is a devotional act. A holy undertaking. Always. Once you are full, an offer of healing to your nearest and dearest will require nothing beyond your presence as you spill over with the energy of universal love. Offer it to the people you pass on the street with just a smile. How deeply do you love yourself? Let the love for others be an outpouring from that, for as you love yourself and awaken, you will recognise there is no self.

An Ode to My Shadow

Hello, beautiful disregarded one. I am sorry I have tried to dismiss you. No longer do I wish to cast you away, deny your existence, reject your presence, or slam the door in your face. I am sorry I haven't wanted to see you.

I see that you are my pain. The suffering I've collected as a human and pushed down to the unconscious. You are the part of me that needs the most love, the most acceptance, the most permission to express yourself – at least to me.

I have spent my life believing you weren't supposed to be here. That belief has only grown as my body has. I believed that you were beneath me, a simple unenlightened noise.

I see you now, dear shadow.

You are me as a little girl. I see that you are innocent. You are me as the teenager who craved belonging; I see that you just wanted to be loved all this time. You are me as a young woman, trying to find her way. I see that you needed me to show you. You look like me as a new mother, with a heart blown open caring for the most precious thing I'll ever have and the sudden anxiety that came along with it. You are the suffering that so often comes with this beautifully uncontrollable human experience and the fear of suffering that was only ever imagined.

You are the wound that never healed. In front of me again, to give me another chance to embrace you, to welcome you in, to become whole. This is all you've ever wanted from me. And you are so patient. My love is all you ever tried to receive, the thing you see me give to others again and again – a witness, an ear, a shoulder, a person that finally understands.

As I take you in my arms, I am truly here for you for the first time. I welcome you. I bring you into my heart, so you may finally know the love that you've always craved. At last I am known fully to myself. I know my highs and my lows. The whole spectrum is seen, the whole thing given permission to exist. I invite you to come home. You are welcome here.

I am whole. I am the love that welcomes all, not by being above it all, but by being the valley beneath to which all flows without discrimination. I am here for you. I am here for me. No part of me is an outcast; nothing is rejected so I am no longer a fragmented being. I scoop up all these forgotten pieces, distortions of the mind, and hold them to my heart for as long as they need holding. And then they let me go.

That's all you ever wanted. To be loved, to be welcomed, to be free.

Compassion is not a relationship between the healer and the wounded. It's a relationship between equals. Only when we know our own darkness well can we be present with the darkness of others. Compassion becomes real when we recognise our shared humanity.

PEMA CHÖDRÖN

Integration

You are an integral part of the whole – the one behind the many. Your life is integrating all that you have become; this is a process.

You are complete, yet always expanding. You can be assured that growth is a constant, and therefore nothing is constant. Even the Source is expanding, growing and reaching.

The limbs of this very Universe are stretching outward. You are becoming more you as you learn to integrate all of what you are. You are the Universe expanding through consciousness.

Feel the years that have brought you precisely to this moment. Feel the centuries of lives that have given this moment the beauty of your presence. Breathe it in.

Chapter 5

Dancing in Duality

The World Before Names

As a little baby, you possessed no language to identify yourself as a separate entity. In the sixth month of your life, you began to see that your mother was a being that was not physically attached to you. Before this understanding, you believed you *were* her – an extension of her, like the thumb of a hand. This early discovery of yourself as an individual sparked your first unsettled belief; this developmental stage is aptly called 'separation anxiety'. From here you entered, with resistance, into a world of concepts and labels. The realm of duality.

In the sky, there is no distinction of east and west; people create distinctions out of their own minds and then believe them to be true.

BUDDHA

The Alchemy of Awareness

Triggers are a stab at an old wound, sacred pointers to our healing. A triggering event shows us where we've been hurt, our tender places. Openings. This opportunity to heal is not for the faint of heart. Sometimes wounds long forgotten – unconsciously buried twenty-plus years ago – will unearth, uproot and expose all the unprocessed pain stored far down in our deepest recesses. As we heal around the recent pain with our fiercely present awareness, memories surface. Out of the darkness, skeletons rise to the light, and only when they've been seen, they finally dissolve into ash. As we witness each layer of wounding, the balm of our consciousness sutures the metaphysical injuries; those holes in our energy receive the medicine of our presence. We cannot heal what we refuse to see. As we open our eyes and bravely hold space for that hurt we've unknowingly carried, we reach into our future self; we unbind our conditioning for that ascended liberation, and we simultaneously ripple healing back to ancestors, generations of wounding unravelling as we find ourselves compassionate. This was all unconscious. None of us knew what we were doing, we operated with inherited illusions and it stops here.

Our healing is the place the story ends. And often it ain't pretty.

The Path of the Spiritual Warrior

The task is not to shield, not to battle, no – but to boldly, courageously witness. This is the path of the spiritual warrior. To hold the truth as the blade and healing as the goal as we stand rooted in our light. In contradiction, although the result heals through the bloodlines and lifetimes, we can only do our work in the here and now. We can gracefully accept the triggers life bestows upon us in real-time as pointers to where healing journeys to next.

In this, we can see those that hurt us as supporting our path, rather than vilified regrets. The button they pushed unlocked the space we were hiding from within ourselves. The most difficult aspect of this hidden space is right in the middle – on a plinth, under a spotlight. We see that, in all of this, we abandoned ourselves. We locked part of us away – the very part that needed us the most. We may experience feelings of remorse. On the other side of that guilt, a promise. A new devotion to self-love. Acceptance.

Our Own Love as Medicine

We see that we really need our own love; that is the medicine. It is also a permission slip to feel it ALL. To experience everything this human experience teaches our spirit. And at last, we embrace our humanity. We accept our pain, our joy, our desires. We love our precious, complicated life. The hidden chamber of shadows, deep underground, receives all the light of our highest love and finally it is cleared in the illumination. We are no longer slaves to fear. We are warriors of love. Unafraid, unashamed, unbound; at last we are whole and free, receiving the majesty of our fathomless love.

We have weathered a storm and witnessed our power, bestowed upon ourselves the gift of being our own sacred guardian, our own best partner. Everything false has collapsed, and we know what remains is true as it vibrates with a harmonious quiver. It was painful but deeply healing to witness the great tapestry of inherited conditioning, held up in front our face by ancestral wounds. Love given under pretence. We assumed that in order to be loved, we needed to give ourselves over to those that didn't value what we attempted futility to cure on their behalf. We understand that our suffering is due to the betrayal of ourselves. We turned our back on our heart, seeking to fill the me-shaped hole with the approval of others. This was a losing game. In claiming our free will, in reclaiming our freedom, this great tapestry of old patterns begins to unravel. Pulling at unconscious strings was unpleasant but inevitable. These strings were cords; each one left us feeling lighter as it tugged away. We cut it all loose, and in our willingness to lose it all, we gained so much – freedom, strength, self-respect. In saying no, we said a big juicy YES to ourselves. This woven patchwork has disintegrated, revealing the true, sweet, good-natured being. And now facing her – seeing her – we have come home to fill that space with the only thing that was ever going to be a perfect fit. We have woken up to where we gave others undeserving authority, and we have cut ourselves loose.

We are free!

We know ourselves. We are strong, sensitive and pure love. We fall in love with her, and we recognise that she is the one for me. We are the guardian of her spirit, the expression of her soul, the embodiment of her love.

Not Mine

Awakening to the True Self, we become aware that another person does not need to affect our emotional state. We detach from the ego of others while becoming more and more aware of our own. We are solely responsible for our own wellbeing. It is here we experience the awareness of the inner world, watching thoughts and emotions flowing endlessly through us like a ceaseless river. These might still be reactive in nature, churning a repetitive story of what must be done in outrage. Drama. We notice there is anger parading as a thought in our mind, demanding attention and staggering through our energy like a drunk who wanders aimlessly and clumsily down the road, unaware of the damage caused. For a long time, we watch, yet still notice the effects and maybe judge ourselves for thinking such things. And then a realisation. The external world does not need to control whether we are happy; we know we can't control it, and we can't control this inner world either! We can be happy regardless of circumstances, regardless of whether we are in or out of control. What could life be like if we lived like that? Is it possible that our joy would be infectious? Wouldn't tending to our own happiness actually be a positive influence on the world around us?

This moment of unconditional joy arose within me one day as I walked through the woods. Previously held emotions and thoughts I'd been struggling to release just let me go, all in one vibrantly translucent moment of clarity. There she was: the awakened one. I was finally left alone as thoughts unthunk me. I stood as the pure self, empty, without resistance. I stopped in mid-stride and laughed at the joke of the mind. Finally, aware that all my suffering had related to having 'my' problems, 'my' thoughts, 'my' emotions – yet these are universal, they don't belong to me. Only in our judgement of them as our own do they linger in our awareness. We don't need to keep them as possessions. When there is no story of *me* and *mine*, there is no suffering. And we are left in awe and perhaps even complete amusement at what our dear mind has been doing.

The mind was just confused believing any of it was real – believing the story belonged to it.

Going Inward

Who is more real? The you that is reading these words, witnessing thoughts parade and come to a pause? Or the thoughts that think you? Can you find the 'I' that worries? Fall back into the arms of the eternal witness. Breathe deep and rest in the nucleus of yourself. See how everything from thoughts to perceptions orbit around you as external phenomena?

Everything That Happens is External

There's the multitude of sense perceptions which enter our mind, and there's the mind which receives the stimuli. One appears internal but if we look deeper, we can see that we aren't the stimuli or the perception of them, but the being beneath the surface. The mind is conceived as a filter for the world to come through, yet still the filter sits outside of our pure, unspoiled awareness. We remain as the inner nucleus. It witnesses the world and the mind's reaction to it. The mind is the space of individualism, our own personal sphere of interpretation. Because the sphere appears unique to us, we believe it is who we are. We listen and believe everything it says. The mind is an atmosphere surrounding the planet we perceive as ourselves. I breathe into my centre. The breath moves through the Earth's atmosphere to touch my aura, my body breathes it in and I follow it beyond the layers into my deep core. There is a deeper self to know beyond the mind.

This is home.
The true *I* is the home.
I am home.

Hall  of Mirrors

The mind is a magnificent teacher, and life is so dream-like because of it. It has a tendency for fear because of its strong preference for love. When we're angry it's because we're not receiving the love that we crave. When we're feeling anything other than joy, we are looking for the external world to give us the reflection of love that we truly are. Yet, as soon as we look with eyes of craving, we are in a space of not seeing the love within, and therefore we don't find it outside of ourselves either. The outside world is only able to reflect us back to ourselves.

We are living in a hall of mirrors.

When we no longer seek for the external world to reassure us or approve of us, we find that we approve of it.

This is how we find peace. This essential, natural state of harmony is our powerful medicine for the shift across humanity. We can only make peace elsewhere when we've laid down the gauntlet in our own head.

When we cease our epic desperation for love out there to fill the in here space, we find such abundant love springing up inside that very space; we find that the space within is entirely love. There is no limit to it, no border around it, no reason for itself except to be there. From here we radiate this love out, and the world will do what it can only, always do: it will reflect that right back.

This is the love that never leaves. The happiness we have pursued. The diamonds we mine are unearthed from the cave of our own sacred heart. That cave will always contain all the riches we could dare to wish for. All right there waiting to be found.

> We are mirrors, receiving ourselves back
> as reflections.

Sometimes we serve as a mirror for a loved one, and in that process, we see in ourselves the dormant volcano, we find the lava-flow beneath our smiling surface. This uncomfortable process is a gift to release buried pain – suppressed anger, grief, fear. We are connected in the sea of life's eternal energy – feeling each other, noticing our buttons being pushed and blaming the other – yet that activated pain only happens when we share a button. We can only trigger in another where we ourselves are triggered. This is an opportunity to become conscious of ourselves. You are alive, experiencing this world through being you – and to the degree you allow yourself to be your Self, is the degree to which life will reflect yourself back to be witnessed. All around, you will find *you* looking back at yourself.

What is a friend? A single soul dwelling in two bodies.

ARISTOTLE

Relating

A tricky topic for most of us is relationships. Our relationships with other. Sooner or later in a long-term friendship or partnership of any kind, we may find ourselves feeling a patch of rather icky feelings. Thoughts of anger separate us from this beloved. Shoulds and shouldn'ts overcome our thought patterns until we may obsessively think of the conflict between ourselves as if we were at war – and it all happens in our head and heart. When we look back over our life, it's things to do with other people that have caused us the most pain, whether that's betrayal, parting ways, or even that inexhaustible journey of pleasing others. Is everything just down to how we relate? If not with another person, with ourselves, with our body, with our work, with our environment? There is a constant push and pull of the internal to the external world. Herein lies the very essence of duality. Relating as one thing to another.

Relationships force us to come up against ourselves. I experienced a time from the vulnerable age of seventeen that I refer to as my Dark Ages. It was in this time I lost my goddess-given ability to speak up, too full of emotion to articulate the voice of rebellion in my head. There it remained for lack of an outlet. I prefer, even now, to saddle the emotion and let its primal energy run me to the hills. I'm simply not a fighter when it comes down to it; I prefer to take flight instead. Whenever I find myself in conflict, I go back to my old way of swallowing truth. This descent is a return to those darker times while all I want is to rise and rid myself of opposition. Is this enlightened? Hardly. Leaving means I win. Confrontation means I lose. What happens then?

These challenges create ripe opportunities for our egos to weaken enough that truth can be ignited. It's not our job to save anybody. It is not our responsibility to make anyone happy, sane, or whole. We can't even make them understand how right we are. What we need to do is not betray ourselves. We listen with earnest to that voice inside our chest, and we become the guardian of its spirit. It might mean we leave people that are impossible to leave. It might mean we stay with people who are difficult to stay with. But we listen to the inner voice above any other. We are the champion of that voice. The only one we can do this for is ourselves.

Who can give me the happy marriage I dream of? Only me. How liberating. I detach from all the noise and I realise I am married to myself.

> Each of our journeys is an articulation of
> the great cosmic energy.

We move through life experience as a collective, under the guise of individuality. Each path is valuable as a worthwhile perspective, yet my interest lies in where the truth is found. I wouldn't dream to think I know your truth. I have no way of knowing the best way for your soul's adventure to play out, even if everyone else would agree on a well-thought-out game plan. I wouldn't be able to judge from my limited human perspective. No one else has been granted access to the ultimate truth of your soul. Only you can visit *that* place and hear *that* voice. It's our greatest work to learn how to listen, to devote ourselves to the inner soul-voice of wisdom. I have found something surprising: when I listen to this voice, its simple direction always benefits the whole. It never concerns itself only with me, it always views the bigger picture and speaks with a precision that is crystal clear.

Perfect Harmony

Heaven is the sea. Where land and ocean perpetually caress, encountering each other with no opinions for how they should be, no need for approval, no desire for love. The two arrive completely as themselves. They exist in perfect harmony.

When I release my narratives about the way I expect you to be, I am free to meet you just as you are – the fresh person you have become.

Without shoulds or shouldn'ts filtering our experience, I need nothing from you – and you then become a crystalline facet of the divine in my experience. A gift. Beautifully expressed divinity. No matter how you are. Clearly you, just as you are. I had been working to create a world that could be coerced into a picture of what I needed it to be, but my mistake was focusing on the image projected rather than the projector. It was my inner mechanisms that needed adjustment all along. Now I need nothing from you, and only now can I share everything with you. I can no more save you than you can save me. How could perfection need saving anyway?

If we suffer, we are lost in shoulds. Without narratives, we feel our way to the truth of things and we find our power. We greet each other fresh as the moment. Inside we find ourselves as radiant beings. No one can take that quality from you. This is the love of your true source – the love of your soul. The love that never leaves.

An Awakened Relationship

Are we in relationships with people or ideas? Can we love unconditionally, or do we love based on whether that person is doing what we believe they are supposed to do so we can be happy?

Am I so weakly rooted in my joy that another's mood can throw me into despair, even anger? That is my wake-up call. My partner has pointed out, in his unwillingness to be what I would call perfect, that I am still asleep at times. My beloved has provoked me to awaken, to ground into myself, to love us both without condition. Am I awake when I need him to change in order to be fulfilled?

The greatest teacher of them all is relationship. It's never about *them* and what *they're* doing. It is always about *you* and what you think about what they're doing.

You don't need to be with a partner who is 'awake' to experience the love of an awakened partnership. If only one of you is awake at any given time that is enough for a perfectly imperfect enlightened relationship.

Even when two enlightened beings come together, their relationship will ebb and flow. Just like the tides, this is the nature of all things. If you wanted perfection, dear heart, you would not have incarnated here. The very fabric of relationships, and indeed life itself, is enriched with stimulating not-perfect challenges. You can count on that.

Give space for each other to be true – true to your own desires, to your own feelings, to your own souls. Honour each other's emotions, cycles and perspectives. Each is valid.

Enjoy quality time together and quality time apart. Be two whole people, not two halves.

Give each other space to grow. Give each other time to work things out. Forgive.

See the other authentically. Look with the eyes of your heart. Love because it is your nature. Love because it feels better than anything else.

Allow love to lead you to where it can express itself.

Don't demand for anything other than truth… and don't ask that your partner change so you might be happy. If they could manage to, it wouldn't last.

Take absolute ownership over your own emotions; those are your sole domain. Do not take responsibility for their emotions; those are theirs to look after.

When you come together, listen to each other. Be there, in that moment, available. Be grateful for a focal point to love with your whole, open heart. And be kind enough to accept love.

An awakened relationship is seeing the
other with the eyes of your heart.

You are made of love. You were made from love. Love is
your truth and your constitution. You don't need another to
experience this, you need only to be in love within yourself
– meaning reside in your heart; this is your crimson womb of
inexhaustible love. Love is what you are.

Who sees all beings in his own self, and
his own self in all beings, loses all fear.

ISHA UPANISHAD

Forgiveness

Forgiveness is an act of self-love.

Forgive to set *yourself* free.

A Self-Love Story

She released the weight of all the ghosts who had wounded her. She let go of those mistakes, those hurts, that she alone had carried.

She was no longer held down. She was now a balloon ascending into the sky. She witnessed herself as a glistening ball of helium, making a run for the stars. She forgave not for their benefit, but to feel the freedom of no longer holding on to pain.

In one moment of realisation she let it all go.

She floated high above gravity's tether.

And she knew what only the birds know.

Going Inward

Write your own forgiveness love story.

What Becomes of the
Wave After it Crashes?

What happened to the infant self I once was? Where did my baby go as he became the little boy he now is?

If I met someone who knew my parents, but hadn't seen me since I was a newborn, they wouldn't be able to stop themselves from speaking of this version of me I don't even remember. They would see me as the grown version of the baby. An image of the past from their minds, a projected history would be who they met. Rather than current me at age thirty-nine, I'd be the newborn in a thirty-nine-year-old body.

I do this with places as well as people. The sight of a giant redwood opens the mental library of images from my honeymoon. The Mediterranean whispers every story my family has passed on from their rich and painful history. The sound of a Swiss-German accent intoxicates my mind with nostalgia for my father's voice, and with it the pang of grief arrives with the provocation. This is how the beautiful mind digests the world as it creates an infinitely complicated collection of narratives wherever it goes.

Our lives are constant rebirths.

Requiring no death, we reincarnate, jumping timelines. The sweetest re-entries are when we arrive fresh – as a soul would land straight into a life memory. When we witness a past life we land square into a moment with no reference points; the narrative just slowly unravels and reveals itself, like a dream with no beginning.

What if I could land fresh into my relationships? No projected memories of who you were yesterday, how we may have been. Rather than forgiving, what if it is as simple as forgetting, arriving here in our brand-new sparkling encounter as two beings who have never truly met before? What if we could meet not as who we've been, but who we are – now, now, now, now, *now*?

Fresh. Reborn. Authentic. Real.

I am not the woman I was yesterday. You might not even be the person you were this morning. Let us meet and see beyond the projection. Let us dare to encounter the depths of each other – beyond story, beyond form, into the clear waters of our true selves. I want to know the true being, here as a pristine soul, alive and reborn in all your glory.

Chapter 6

The Temple
of the Heart

The Trinity

The soul births into being the body and mind at once. The divine trinity is made manifest as the multi-faceted being that you are. In Christian terminology this is described as the father, the son and the holy spirit. In meeting the son, you are guided to the father. In other words, in meeting your soul, you are guided to Source. Your soul is the guru. Buddhists recognise three jewels: the Buddha (awakened one), the dharma (the practice) and the sangha (the community of practitioners). The Hindus illustrate this idea through the Trimurti: Brahma, Vishnu and Shiva – representing the cycle of creation, preservation and destruction. In Reiki it is understood as the three diamonds: from Oneness is born the Earth (form) and the heavens (formless). The original energy manifests simultaneously into two expressions and the triangle of our divine life is born.

The body and mind are created together as manifestations of the soul – just as left and right are conjoined twins. We can't experience one without creating the other. This is duality. And it is also the salvation of co-being. The path back to our Source. When we realise this deep truth of inter-being, we find an opportunity for liberation.

Everything is Connected

A cornerstone of Buddhist philosophy is the understanding that everything is connected; nothing in the Universe can exist independently. The daughter cannot exist without the mother. We can't take the oak tree out of the acorn. Not only that, we can't remove a single event from our ancestors' lives prior to the conception of a distant grandparent. Every single bit of them, including their decisions, their challenges and their preferences, is wrapped up in our existence. Being here at this precise moment depends on each strand of DNA that evolved on Earth to create the blueprint of humanity. Even deeper than that, we depend entirely on the unique unfoldment of the Universe to have happened as it happened. We are born of our ancestors – born of their energy, their genes, their blood, their culture. Our bodies are made of stardust. We have ancestors in mineral, vegetable, animal, human and celestial forms. We cannot separate ourselves from any of them; they inhabit every cell of our body as a continuum of life. Each of their experiences are inseparable aspects leading to the divine manifestation of you.

I am made of many things that are not me. The rose is not just the rose, but many things that are not categorised as the rose. The sun, the soil, everything that decomposed to create the soil, the rain (made of rivers, oceans and clouds), the mother plant, her grandmother, the pollen, the bees, the gardener. In just the sunlight that nurtured her, we can trace our rose's connection to the Milky Way and the nebulous cloud of cosmic dust that created our solar system. All these non-rose elements make it possible for the rose to be a rose. She could not exist in space alone.

To gaze upon a flower deeply enough, we find the entire Universe alive in her perfume.

The Earth is not existing independently of you. You are co-being with her, she is alive within your body. Together-being. If you're able to connect to your inter-being with the environment around you – sun, air, food, water – then through the environment you can find your connection to every other being through all of time. Even just by following your breath out and in – notice how it connects you to the trees, to all other living things and beyond.

If I am Reiki and you are Reiki, then we must be the same. We must also be within each other.

The mind is born in a peaceful home. It journeys into the world, gets lost and finds suffering. In the confusion, its way is forgotten – but all it ever needs to do is return home to the heart. The body is the anchor for the mind to find the soul. Our holy ground. Our temple.

The Axis of Our Being

The heart knows only of infinite, sacred abundance. Its natural state is open beyond open. When told the story of less, the nervous system rebels. The true heart is expansive – an everlasting horizon where Earth and sky kiss. It beats with electrical stardust. The measurement of its height and depth are both limitless.

In the heart we experience the marriage of our two aspects – the union of the human and the being. The external and internal worlds gather in this meeting space we know as home. It is here we blend heaven and Earth, soul and body. This is where our divinity as the unmanifest essence meets its physical counterpart – the manifest aspect of our impermanence. Everything relates to everything else within this coalescing space. The axis of our being.

The heart is where reality collapses in on itself and from where it all expands out. This is our personal convergence of Big Bang energy. Some physicists imagine that one day, the Universe will have expanded out to its farthest possible expression and then begin its return journey inwards; a collapse of space will fall back into its heart until it's once again an unimaginably small speck of infinitely concentrated energy. We currently ride along its bellowing outward breath, expanding with the fabric of space before it breathes the return inhalation. This cosmological theory is called the Big Bounce. If it is true, we have no way of knowing how many times the Universe has expanded and retreated to begin this process again. If this is but one exhalation, how many breaths has it made? Can we see that we live like this too?

Centred from the heart – the first organ that comes alive within our mother's womb – we grow and expand. We exist as stardust that has inexplicably become a person with the potential for awakened consciousness. And then we reach a point in our manifest expression of our pinnacle – the farthest we can express in body – and we make the journey back to our centre point into the pure divinity from which we arose. Expansion back to contraction, to then expand again and again. For what purpose other than the delight of this dance we do not know. This is all a journey in and out of the heart. Our heart is the heart of creation. We breathe ourselves in and out of unity consciousness.

We know the Universe is not eternal, because it is manifest. It has form and can therefore cave in on itself or reach a point of its expansion where it has thinned out too much, causing it to freeze. Consciousness, however, is not manifest, it is timeless. It is the mysterious creative intelligence behind all this magic; consciousness is an intrinsic quality of existence. Within the realm of our heart, we experience our relationship to this very physical place, and we feel the miracle of our fleeting existence. This organ is the first in the body to be created, and its last beat will coincide with our last breath. Its aliveness is vital to our existence. We are both impermanent human and eternal being all at once. The breakable and the unbreakable. Our fullness is realised when we live as fully embodied souls, expressing ourselves from this vast open space of pure energy, right in the middle of our chest. Grounded into our fullness so that any external energy is only witnessed, rather than inhabited as interference.

The heart is where duality is reconciled.

If we agree with this model of the Universe, we can see how everything surrounding us came to be from the smallest little seed of pure potential. This singular seed of energy sprouted into the Universe with the Big Bang. If this is the heart of the entire Universe, the soul of which is Source itself, imagine this heart has expanded to give us life. We are in the heart as fragments of the infinite heart, to experience ourselves as conscious points of perspective. Our greatest purpose is to focus, to come into the moment completely, living in pure delighted harmony with the present, and to awaken to this miracle of life. How could we not be madly in love with being alive?

As we journey into our heart, we meet
the essence of the Universe.

The whole awakened self is who we really are – the True Self. This pilgrimage is a return journey, taking us home to the realm of our soul – the inner sanctuary of the heart. Breathe in.

Carry your heart through this world like a life-giving sun.

HAFIZ

Guardian of the Soul

I am the gatekeeper of the soul. The portal to the realm of pure being. I am ever expansive, forever opening to allow more of myself to touch the world around me. I am the bridge between the heavens and this Earth. I am vastness. I am life.

I am the wisdom-keeper. The springboard to knowledge, the anchor of soul memory, the seer of truth.

I witness the passing clouds. I remember all the journeys in and out of myself. I recall all the people that have enriched my knowing of myself and all the rawness of being human. The scars give me character. I can never be broken but I have stretched beyond my comfort many, many times.

I feel the rain, the starlight upon me, the breath in me that surrounds me as the wind. I feel the Earth as the love that envelopes me. I sense the presence of Gaia, my beloved mother who makes my next breath possible. I touch the heart of all beings in fearlessness. I am safe in my vulnerability, for I know myself as all. I sense the fear around me, but I am unafraid, for I see beyond the distortion.

I contain the infinite riches of your inner wealth. This treasure store is yours alone, it can never be taken from you and it cannot be earned. This immense abundance is yours to access through cultivating presence, living with loving kindness for yourself and others, watering seeds of gratitude and expressing joy for the miracle of life. Your reverence for all living beings makes the riches grow and spill out to all that pass you.

My natural dwelling place is full of a non-discriminating love for all beings. My love is unconditional.

My beat is in rhythm with the Universe. My nature is to come back to balance. I will always course-correct towards harmony.

In the deeper recesses of my inner chambers, I remember that we may seem two, but we are not. There seems an up and a down, but that's only a way for us to name the world. I connect the dots to realise there are no dots.

I am your guide, your friend, your life-force. I am your temple, my beloved one.

Love the One You're With

Love the one you're with. That's you.

In loving yourself with all your heart, you discover your immense capacity for love. You realise what a joy it is to be you and awaken to what a blessing it is to get to be with yourself every day. In this love, your essence is realised. You look back over your childhood and you say sweetly to that younger, innocent self, 'I've always been with you. I love you.'

Your normal self-talk becomes gracious, grateful, soft. You allow yourself to be perfectly human – a perfect soul with permission to live an imperfect life. Loved more so for every so-called imperfection.

You can be you, enough as you are, lovable as you are – loving yourself just because. Your internal dialogue grows kind, and your body relaxes in the gentle approval and appreciation you now offer.

Because the whole wide world is a mirror, it too shifts to reflect this growing love of yourself. You now know you are worthy of it and receive it with open arms. Validation arrives from the centre of your soul and here you become a devotee to this, above all else. You honour its *yes* and you honour its *no*. You rediscover the precious ease of living in harmony with your sacred self. And you may then see there was never a self at all.

As you become your own best friend, life becomes the most generous companion. Softly, and with no judgement at all, it kindly delivers all you ask for, mirroring the relationship you have with it. The language it understands is your emotion. So, if you have an emotion you want to transmute, try to simply allow it, and then try loving it – love every part of your deep, deep self. You are worthy of your own great love. There is no more potent medicine than that. You don't need to get rid of anything; rather, that thing is a lost part of yourself asking to be embraced. To become whole. Surrender to it by giving it your full attention, as if it was your sweet baby crying with all her might. Discover what you need to feel safe again.

You are your soul mate, the one you've been wanting to know your whole life. She was waiting for you, right in the depths of your own heart. In the reunion, you are whole.

You wander from room to room hunting for the diamond necklace that is already around your neck.

R U M I

You Are Enough

How could you not be? You are a living miracle. A unique soul, energy expressed as this shape and form we know as you. Nature never makes mistakes; it creates, evolves, reinvents, each creation more perfect than the last. Do you think you weren't included in this process?

There is a vast container of intelligence within you, a portal to any answer you seek. It pulses in the centre of your chest. You do not need another person to validate you, you do not need any outside opinion – whether from a guide, angel, audience, beloved friend on Earth, or any book – the only one to follow is that wise being in your heart. Your work is to listen to it, attune your mind to the frequency of your heart. Let that truth bubble up and out; let it be known to you and vocalised without censorship. You are made of love, full of elements from stars, as life itself – right here. As you. If that wisdom scares you, yet somehow opens your heart, it's true. If your chest tightens or recoils, it's false. How simple it is to see where the mind is identified. How does that thought feel? Is it true?

Going Inward

You can use this heart response to check in with yourself about any decision you might be trying to make. Notice where the energy goes – do you spin out in doubt or confusion? Does the idea lift your energy and bring thoughts of freedom?

When we're in crisis we want nothing more than to feel better. We reach for change, find reasons for why we suffer. But we can sit with the suffering, look at the beliefs that hold the suffering world in orbit and ask those beliefs how true they are. We don't need to suppress a thing, we can be grateful for every thought that arises; our arms are open to sit with ourselves – to heal and work with our mind, rather than strike futility against it. That is self-love. Unafraid of anything our mind does, we gently, kindly, unconditionally offer our love to each thought. We invite our mind round for supper, sit with any belief that limits our experience and love each one back to truth.

Darling, is that true? Is that what you want to believe? Does that thought expand your world or make it smaller?

I welcome you, darling heart. I welcome you too, ego-mind. Let's sit together and find the truth of the soul as our guiding light. Let's align ourselves with light and work together in service to it. Nothing could be sweeter than flowing in harmony together – knowing we can face whatever comes. Knowing that life is kind, the Universe friendly and our true nature loving. We can only truly know ourselves once we've reconciled our many dimensions and become whole.

Wholeness becomes possible when we welcome all of ourselves to the table, without judgement or fear. We give ourselves the love we have been so hungry for.

Connected

A client came to see me feeling outside of her relationship to her husband, to her friends, to her child and to her life. Whenever we came back round to the relationship that she had with herself, she'd cry. This is the most important one we have and perhaps the most frequently neglected. I encouraged her to spend some time connecting back with herself, and with very wet cheeks, she asked, 'How?' How do we connect to ourselves when we feel lost? This question contains a false premise, but it reveals the most prevalent starting point of suffering amongst almost everyone: there are two selves, and they don't always seem to be getting along. We are a human and a being, and our purpose is being human. This has been depicted in mythologies, in classic pairings of archetypes – that image we all recognise of the devil and angel in miniature, whispering in either ear. One softly shares wisdom, while the other is concerned with its own small self. We are a soul embodied, with a mind that's been conditioned before we were wise to conditioning.

You can never not be yourself, just as the wave can never not be water. We often believe a flawed idea that tells us otherwise. How do you get back in touch with the core essence of who you really are? You make time for yourself, like you would make time for a relationship you want to heal.

You carve time from your busy life tending to everyone else, and you breathe into your centre. You act kindly to yourself. You make this single relationship your priority. There are always these two beings – the human and the soul – and the soul is there to love you. Let it.

I have witnessed a theme flowing through the paths of many, as they unravel concepts unquestionably adopted as their own. These false concepts become the lens that the mind sees through, and these ideas of not being worthy *as we are* become the baseline vocabulary of our inner dialogue. As we wake up and notice the dialogue has a voice of its own, we have an opportunity to recognise that voice is not ours. It comes from the confusion perched on our shoulder. It might sound like a critical parent – no doubt an echo of a grandparent – a reverberation of unconscious thought patterns. This foreign energy builds obstacles between us and ourselves. Who is that self we are reaching for? It's that essence of pure love that occupies the deep well of our inner heart. It's the part that hears the critical echo but doesn't listen to it. It's the wisdom that compassionately questions how true any of that chatter really is. This is the self we long to know, to cherish and to foster a more authentic relationship with. So how do we do that? We notice our humanity by giving ourselves the space to pull back from it.

Theta State

When I receive Reiki, I notice that my body has fallen asleep, but I am simultaneously fully conscious. This is the magical state known as *Theta*. While my body is deeply resting, my mind is somehow *still* thinking, yet me, as my

True Self, is pure delighted, soft, beautiful awareness – taking all of it in with as much interest and presence as ever. Not thinking but *being thought* – the field unto which the thoughts parade past. I'm aware that there is a surface to this deep oceanic space of consciousness, full of choppy thought waves, and yet I am far below it, looking up to the light dancing through the water, completely submerged in my truth and my peace.

We simply need space. Space to feel that real understanding of who we are, to surrender our identity as the unconscious voice in exchange for the bliss of pure being. You can't be disconnected to your True Self because that is who you are. You might believe the thought that you're disconnected, but that doesn't make it true. Who had that thought? You are simply identified with the idea that you're apart. Which of those voices is capable of this idea?

Going Inward

If you are feeling out of sync with yourself, just notice which aspect you've become closer with. Sit in silence and let yourself sink into the depths of your inner heart as you take in one large breath; the blissful expanse of pure beingness hasn't gone anywhere.

Drop into your heart and say to it: Thank you for unravelling all that is not true, so what is true may be revealed. Thank you for the deep, deep healing that these threads weave. Thank you for taking away all that is false so I may see my true, naked self in all her magnificence! Thank

you for revealing to me where I need healing;
as the light of consciousness fills my life, the
shadows are illuminated and fade from existence.

And so it is.

In the depth of winter, I finally learned that within me there lay an invincible summer.

ALBERT CAMUS

The Heart Sutra

To have it all, we must be willing to lose it all. To lose our need to be right. To lose our need for approval. To lose the illusory sense of our mind-made self – the separate entity that we identify as. We release it all to the great abyss in order to find we are the entirety of it all. We aren't right as an ego but right as the whole one mind. Our lives become right in our relinquishing of any control, any desire to prove, any reflex to defend or define ourselves.

We spend most of our adult lives accumulating – knowledge, money, things, relationships – and then fear the loss of these things as loss of ourselves. We become attached to what surrounds us as a means to grasp hold of what we are – the ungraspable essence. Born naked, free, alive into wonder, we find ourselves fully clothed, identified as this or that – a personality existing with self-imposed limitations.

And then one unexpected, unassuming day, without any announcement, you touch the shore. You retreat back as the wave. And in that movement, back into the sea of life, you realise there was never a shore. Far below you, under the depths of the ocean is earth. You've been passing between what appeared to you as separate lands but, in fact, they were always connected. There is no getting there. There is no over there. There is nothing to reach for, nowhere to go. It was only a thought that classified places apart, as destinations to pursue. Then you find yourself upon the shore again. Deliciously bathing in the warmth of presence. The second you conceptualise it, or desire to hold on to it, the sea pulls you back. Then you wonder, was there ever a shore? Was there ever a *me*? And you release the dream, sinking deeper into your nature, into pure awareness. A being onto which life dances.

Surrender to the Depths

I had one of those fantastically vivid dreams last night, and waking from it I realise that dream was as real as any of my thoughts. Past, future, memories – all manifest outside the moment, in a sleeping state. This activity is the mind making sense of the world, attempting to comprehend the vastness of life. We have this tool to make anything we like in life; humans seem to have a proclivity for suffering, but when we lose the need for holding onto anything for fear of suffering, we are left with a still, bottomless, sweet-tasting sea of joy. That joy is constantly present, just waiting for the mind to part its persistent curtains long enough. The mind outwardly seeks to return to the space of its source, not realising that it merely has to surrender to the very depths from which it arose in order to experience the very thing it wants most of all. Suffering is born out of our need to control and change the world. The only aspect of this world we can change is ourselves – our mind. We can only change the world by changing our mind. This undiluted sea of joy is a conscious presence. I call it 'soul' yet it is beyond names – the eternal dwelling place of our True Self. Our home. Our freedom.

The mind sprouts out from this home to explore the endless possibilities of its own imaginings, an entirely projected reality we experience as life. What it actually wants is the experience of joy from which it came – the essence of itself. This joy springs from its own roots, rather than raining down from outside of itself. This is why happiness has absolutely nothing to do with our external world, and why our whole world naturally shifts when we return our focus to the source from which we came, from the infinite space within ourselves.

We have the power to experience anything we can imagine; indeed just imagining something is an experience of the thing. Try imagining anything at all and you will find your body is flooded with a verification of this experience as reality, a chemical response to the dream. In anticipation of being tickled, we feel it happening, we squirm and laugh. This intelligence is built into our system. We have the homing device that beckons us with the pulse of joy. Anything less is a signal that we've got turned around. We merely have to sink into its embrace to discover the treasure we have worked so hard to excavate. It was always within us, just beneath the surface.

Our mind gifts us with a dream world to play out, a universe of possibilities to enjoy or not, for we have the freedom to choose. Awareness is the key to it all. Joy is the surest guide. Follow the light that joy shines and you will find yourself floating across the great abyss, safe on the raft that is your soul.

Chapter 7

The Ecstatic Void

The Persistent Silence

There is a persistent silence that precedes all sound. The still void holds each sound as a wave that passes through it. You can't get behind the silent canvas. In the same way, it is our consciousness that holds space for every thought, every experience and every emotion to pass through. Our pure being, this background containing self, is the first, and last, instance to any circumstance. We can't get behind it. When you sink far back enough or become still in that deepest of places, you'll find no boundary to it – no time, no point in space that it occupies, for it is space itself. This pure being exists before thought, identity, or any concept of itself as a this or that. It is the field of timeless awareness. It's the mind's woke eye as a screen for dreams. This is your true being, the nameless one I call Source or soul.

If you let yourself, you'll realise it was always there beneath every experience as the focal point where all lines converge, just as the silence is there under every sound. When you find the sweet abyss of this place, I'll meet you there, for here we are one and the same. When you touch this place, as far back from your identified self as you can go, you may feel it as the blanket of darkness that holds the light – the void of black which gives way for stars. We are only scared of darkness because we fear that unknown territory where all edges collapse. Where our mind gives way from being a thing, to being the no-thing-ness that holds it all together.

Let's meet there. I'll be the one smiling without a face.

The Finger and the Moon

There is a Zen parable that says: the finger pointing at the moon is not the moon. Meaning, do not mistake the teachings that lead to awakening for awakening itself. At some point, your eyes must leave their contact with the finger and move across the void towards the moon. When I point outside to a squirrel so our little cat can enjoy the sight of the furry passerby, the cat doesn't look outside. He looks at my finger, and sometimes he licks it, but he always misses the squirrel.

If we want to find our True Self, we must release our focus from the teaching that leads us there and just *be* there. To see the luminous sphere, you must leave the realm of concepts and shift into another space. As such, this work is a bridge to help you cross to the other side and, once across, leave the bridge and explore the moonlit land that awaits you. Sometimes the finger points and you look, only you still do not experience the lunar event – are you looking for it with an active mind? Is it a new moon, hiding itself?

Being Without Thought

The first time I caught a glimpse of that elusive moon I was crossing London Fields at sunrise, after a lively night at a house party. This was not my most spiritual state, and I would not have planned it this way, but it was the first time I experienced delicious being without thought. Leaving the comforting warmth of that party with all its music and energy, I stepped outside where it was cool and quiet. There was a mist hugging the ground in perfect stillness. The sudden shift of atmosphere took my mind along with it. I became totally present for the first time, aware of the world all around me – the world outside my head. I heard each leaf as a roaring ocean in the many plane trees that line that park. My senses were heightened. I noticed the totality of the moment. This was a mini-awakening; I was aware of being aware. For all appearances, I had accidentally slipped into a parallel dimension.

Each time we enter presence, we step into an adjacent reality – one which existed all along yet had been completely unknown to us from the other side, that familiar side of mental noise. Entering presence is intensified when shared with other beings. Noticing flowers, trees, and animals occupying the present makes the connection to our true nature much deeper. When my mind isn't distracting me from it, I'm in their world as my natural self – watching, being, without any need to control or change what life is naturally doing. I'm alive to it all and so very pleased to be. There is a sweet awesomeness to this plane of existence – a dreamlike experience when it happens, where the only thought, which arises as an awareness, is, 'I'm here.' This follows with a game of concentration, as if swimming amongst fish in total awe to be in their world, holding the breath for as long as possible. From the everyday thought-fuelled existence this seems like a true miracle, and once we arrive, it just *is* – the way things are.

Trying to describe this state reminds me of the futility of a perfume advert. No matter how striking or how long it runs for, the celebrity-starring film-noir campaign gives me no idea of the fragrance. I will only know it by inhaling the scent for myself.

There's space to be here. Space to notice the richest, most minute details of life, details we simply miss in the sleeping world because our mind is full of thought – often stressful, repetitive chatter that pushes us to run this way and that. Here, instead, we are the awareness. We are home in ourselves. This is the vantage point of our soul – the pure, divine, aware consciousness that we really are. This is why it's called *awakening*, because when you suddenly find yourself aware of life in all its many glories, you realise you had been sleeping your way through it up until that moment. We had no idea we were dreaming all that time, until we sat bolt upright to see the world just as it is, free of the narrator's voice in our head. Being alive, we witness life being life, and we are overwhelmed with love for it all. We are awake.

An Expression of Source

We may then realise that Source is All That Is. Logically, All That Is *is* everything, meaning the good, the bad, the ugly; the manifested and the unmanifested potential, the high and the low, the joy and the suffering, the enlightened and the tormented – both finger and moon. The one that knows nothing of Source is still part of All That Is due to the very nature of being *All That Is*. You can never be separate from Source, therefore, everything you do is an expression of Source. This means something altogether more significant: there is no wrong way to live. Life appears to be a grand experiment where all results are worthy because they shed light in some way. Experiments are how we gather information, how we learn. All of life must therefore be fulfilling its purpose. You can't do anything wrong. You've never made a mistake. Your entire life has been a journey of becoming, evolving and experiencing life.

> The smack-me-on-the-forehead,
> so-profoundly-obvious purpose of
> being alive is... to live!

> *That* is a miracle.
> That is freedom.

You, dear soul, are acting out your life just the way you are meant to. The fact that you are alive is a sacred pact in action. This knowing dawned on me while I sat on a train, on an ordinary Thursday afternoon on my way to watch a film about Thich Nhat Hanh in Piccadilly Circus. By the time it was over, I had cried the sort of tears that only come on the crest of great relief. I exited the cinema in a state of the deepest presence I had yet encountered. A joy grew upwards from the very roots of my being, the foundations of consciousness. I saw life all around me. It was miraculous. It was being done in the most accurate way that it could be done. Every person fulfilling their destiny, just by being here. We run around looking for the purpose of life, all the while its purpose has been satisfied every moment of every day.

Life is Source experiencing All That Is. What a thing to realise. You are doing this right. You cannot do this in any other way.

The path of awakening is not about
becoming who you are. Rather it is about
unbecoming who you are not.

ALBERT SCHWEITZER

The Many Worlds of You and Me

All change is made when we shift perspective. When we do this, we rise up into clarity.

There exist within me many worlds; some are low, dark places. When I take residence in the lower dimensions of myself, I suffer. I believe my needy thoughts, I judge, I blame, I plot escape routes. When this underworld releases me, I begin to float to my higher world – the realm of clarity, blue skies, joy. The thoughts here are less frequent, and when they come, they talk of pleasant things. I am independent, empowered, free. No need to escape a thing; rather, this me offers an ecstatic embrace, without any clinging or desire for alterations. The me I become in this world loves purely and moves effortlessly as things come and go. She knows better than to identify with the external world as her source of happiness. She flows with it, guided by inner wisdom. She's connected.

I have many worlds within myself – some call this heaven on Earth; some call it hell. I see that this is true for all human beings. We ride waves of frequencies and we have this sublime power called free will. We can visit any world, any reality we so choose. We are many worlds amongst many worlds, colliding in universal orbits, creating moons in our wake.

Seeing Our Lives as Perfectly Right

What is real? The me without judgement. The projector, before it projects. The world of stillness that holds the space for the rest. Peace, clarity – I find these friends by saying goodbye to my ego, that phantom self that limits my perspective. Sometimes this means it needs to crumble. That can be painful as the grip comes apart and I fall into a bottomless place, until I realise this is the freedom I have always sought. Nothing can hold me, and I surrender. The fall becomes the flight.

To believe we *need* the world to be any different from what it is, is insanity. It is here as it is. You are here, as you are, and I am here just the same. We are ever-changing, evolving things. Peace is accepting this moment (and all of its inhabitants) to be as it is. From this bliss of honouring reality, we find a love beyond acceptance. We discover wells of joy, outpourings of gratitude. We see our lives are perfectly right. And we find ourselves enlightened. For the moment. We can see each other as works in progress. Humanity is not finished yet.

We are caretakers of the mind. We can only seek to care for our direct self. In doing so we can then take care of the One self. Moving from control to grace, we have no say in anything outside of ourselves. We can only offer pure love by loving ourselves as another. This honours everyone else's choices, their decisions, their perspective of the dream.

Going Inward

What is true? Universally, true in the absolute? Allow the answer to bubble up, not as a thought to be thunk, but rather a knowing to rise. Ride that to the surface and breathe the soft, salty air that refreshes you in this transcendent world. This is the atmosphere that surrounds all the other worlds. It holds it all together. You might experience a vacuum as you wake up; it's a rush of space/time as you make your ascension beyond the illusory.

What transcends all worlds? The nameless being that moves through them.

A Taste of Enlightenment

Last night I tasted enlightenment. I released it all. There was no pain, no problem, nothing but sheer beauty.

My son was in the bath. As I was kneeling by the tub, washing him, my mind drifted to contemplate the 'Origins' text in the following chapter. This hypothesises that during the moment of the Big Bang, Source fragmented, becoming all the perspectives of the Universe in order to know and experience itself. As I thought about this beautiful idea, I heard an inner whisper: *you* experiencing *yourself*. As these words were transmitted, my crown opened so wide it was as if I no longer possessed a head. This message zapped me from the conceptual to the visceral.

> I am Source experiencing itself.
> You are Source experiencing itself.

I as you, you as me.

Truthfully, there is no 'me', there is no 'you'.

With this went my identity as a separate self. Little me was no more. I was just there, consciousness staring in awe at my son as he became a joyous example of Source experiencing life, and I along with him. Nothing existed outside that moment. Nothing other than that bathroom was real or in my awareness. It was pure focus, free from the strain of concentration.

We talk about Source as if Source *isn't* us – but we are a part of it; it's alive *as* us. We are Source having an experience. Us. As Source. Right now.

As I sat there, watching my son play, many minutes of complete wonder ticked by. I recall saying 'wow' as I held this state of pure bliss. I looked into his warm green eyes with joy for this perspective. Touching his little foot, I felt myself touching my own foot. I felt it as my own. When I finally spoke, my voice was someone else's; I had an awareness behind the vibration of it. I was deep inside my own body listening to an outside noise. It was similar to the scene in *Being John Malkovich* when Cameron Diaz's character witnesses John's life from within his body. I was the extreme witness, far in the background, watching. No longer really an 'I' but rather just a thing, a place, a fascinated audience.

At bedtime, it takes a little negotiating to get Elias into his pyjamas, we read a few stories and I typically sing lullabies until he falls asleep. On this night, I dressed him without any effort. All was peaceful; our movements into bed were effortless. I placed my hand on his head, gave him Reiki for no more than two minutes and he quickly fell into a deep sleep. No song was sung. No fuss was made.

I returned to the bathroom to brush my teeth. Nothing in the world existed apart from this marvellous little room. I felt immense gratitude for the toothbrush and the toothpaste that 'old me' had left for the me that was present that day.

'Old me' was the me I had identified with from only a limited perspective. On this day, for the first time, I really saw her. She was kind. She took care of me, leaving offerings to cleanse myself with. I felt like her guest and was honoured to be staying in her home. I was filled with immense appreciation for what she does for me, all without a thought for what she's doing for me. I noticed the little pot of face cream, and I saw a woman who loved herself. She was so good at being alive. This was her purpose.

Every noise, every scent, every object is an expression of divinity. Life being life. This state of stillness, which possessed a fascination for it all, stayed with me until I woke up the next morning, back to being me. Me as Brighitta. A spark of the one containing the many, as one of the many.

There is no story in the present moment. No pain, no drama to play out, no grudges, or anything at all to consider. With Elias in that bath there was nothing in the world to focus on – and nothing would have been near as precious. Those old narratives that began with 'I need' and 'I want' ceased – and when I looked, I found they were all created from a dark little room under the stairs of my awareness. They were false trappings of a human, stubbornly identified as her thoughts. Hypnotised by the concepts in her mind, fixated on a small piece of the expansive picture.

Those limiting stories seem to be as rational as the tip of my little finger being angry at the index finger, needing to be told it was worthy of love from the hand, or craving to be positioned in the middle, or at the wrist – believing it could ever be anything other than hand as a whole and body beyond.

We are an undulating network of minds fresh under amnesia – asleep to the one consciousness, the expanding Universe. I can sense that little me who hides in the dark is still there. I can go stroke her hair, ask her to play and watch her retreat again, and then I can climb the stairs once more to the light of truth. If she can be there, and I can be here, I must not be her. She's my human identity. She's my phantom self – an illusion. She's there to teach me all the ways of this world and species – all aspects of the broader me, the broader you.

All of the people in your life allow you to know life, to know God/Spirit/Source as fully as you are able. Every being on this Earth is a molecule of the divine. When you look at another, you look at yourself. Everyone is you, looking back at you. Just as you can't separate the various notes that blend to create a harmony, you can't be separate from the Source of All That Is. Our tones surrender to union simply by our existence. You might fall out of key, but you can vibrate right back to harmony by dropping any story that feels otherwise.

Now I watch the world with wide eyes. Look at all we are capable of – what a range of emotion and thought! We occupy a sea of sheer beauty as all the elements, all the frequencies, all the states of dreaming and wakefulness. I love every particle. This is us, knowing us.

> We are each a sacred breath of the divine,
> flowing through the air of All That Is.

Enlightenment is intimacy with all things.

JACK KORNFIELD

The Moment

I feel thirsty. I lift the glass of water from the table and take a sip. The person that reached out to raise the glass is gone. I let the cool liquid move through my mouth, as if it's the first time I've ever tasted water. It hydrates all the crevices it can find before I drink it in. I release the glass back to the table. The version of me that put the glass down has already dissolved.

The me that wrote those words has vanished without a trace. What remains but the infinite unfolding? The newly arrived unborn moment. Dying within its own birth, it stays for an infinity. Impermanence is our greatest ally. By giving us nothing it provides everything. Each freely passing moment arrives in its complete beauty. It can no more be held than the breath.

There is nothing to hold. The attempt makes us tense in our desire for stability but there is no ground to stand on. We are free. Free to narrate, to fly, to fall, to create, to be like the wind on its journey to I-know-not-where. The freedom that arrives and moves through us is our very essence.

With the next breath, we are created anew. A wave of beingness with no destination. What remains is the essential unseen.

The being that is. It witnesses the thirst and the grace of the water. It notices the generosity of life. It rests in its own ungraspable presence. It arrives just as it passes.

Ku

The immeasurable field of pure beingness arises as the dimension of *Ku* that the Buddhists speak of. Remember the first symbol, *Cho Ku Rei*? This is the emptiness it was pointing us towards. The power turns on when the mind lets go.

This translates as the sacred clarity we can hope to touch upon in deep states of meditation. The emptiness isn't a negative thing like an empty glass. Rather it is an open mind unencumbered by duality, sensing everything merged into the One-Space, free of concepts with nothing to grasp or attach to. The place from which all arises and to which it all returns. Have you ever noticed the deliciousness of your mind when it's empty of thought? It is absolutely peaceful as soon as it pauses. And when there is no thought filling our awareness, we are suddenly able to receive unimaginable amounts of sacredness from the moment. We can deepen our connection to Reiki and bring more energy into our sessions.

Going Inward

Ku is the cosmic void. To enter it, you simply go backwards in your awareness as far as you can reach. Dip far beneath thoughts, into the space behind them. Reading this now you may have briefly gone there – the still point, the most peaceful centre of yourself. You'll know when you reach it.

In glimpses of surrendering to the ultimate self, where truth is absolute, the ego identity called 'personality' will begin to dissolve as your true identity emerges. Enlightenment is the absence of identification; that is the emptiness of *Ku*. You'll enter what feels like a tunnel of some kind as an immense force pulls you towards awakening. You'll glimpse such vastness that your mind may be terrified as the ultimate encroaches onto the dream we call reality, tugging at the seams. And if you should find yourself clutching at the familiar parameters of life's grand illusion, this is okay too. We are alive in bodies after all – a face of Source, having its life as the Universe, as this person in this miraculous body, on this world we call home. But should you continue beyond the tunnel, you will find the sweet abyss. The entirety of you. The limitless field of energy we call Source. This background awareness is the precursor to everything, the field that life plays out upon. You're not in any way separate from it, you're an extension of it. You've arisen from it as a wave upon the endless sea. When you gaze out upon the vastness of *Ku*, you know this as truth.

The void isn't nothingness, it's the open state. The canvas. Pure consciousness. Possibility. The silence in which sounds emerge from and disappear to. *Ku* is the divine energy of spaciousness. Space without time.

The mind in its enlightened state is blissful openness; it's empty like a cloudless sky. When the mind rests, it is deliciously clear and available to life. It receives insights, it knows, it is awake to itself. As Reiki practitioners working with other people, it's the best quality we can offer – being the empty vessel for Reiki to pour through, unobstructed by judgements or concepts. Most new practitioners want to do the opposite; we want to jump into the healing session with our mind. We want to know what a certain feeling indicates, what it all means, how we can shift the energy, what to do, what to say afterwards. This comes from our habit of needing to *do* the healing, rather than *be* the healing. We want to embody this state of *Ku* so the intelligence of pure undiluted soul can flow freely, enabling our client to touch upon the vastness of their potential. We don't have to do a thing.

We cannot get behind consciousness. Everything that we talk about, everything that we regard as existing, postulates consciousness.

MAX PLANCK

Formless Intelligence

We are movement through space as undiluted consciousness. Nothing needs to be said. No words convey the essence that transcends language.

The formless intelligence glimpses itself. Without judgement, without distraction, without time, it arises from its own source. The infinite field onto which all plays out and all the players that are playing.

It moves in all directions from its centre and discovers there is nowhere that *it* is not. It listens to buzzing silence as it drinks in life. It passively receives the whole Universe, as the sea accepts all of the rivers – flowing towards the source from which they all came.

There is no time, only thoughts of time.

The linear focus of past/future halts in one breath and turns on its axis. Perception becomes vertical, an enticing exploration of boundless depths and unspeakable heights. Our attempt to capture the cosmos only demonstrates that it is an expanded tapestry of time as a whole – only ever occupying a single moment. The twinkling lights arrive to meet our eyes after travelling for millions of light-years – extensions of their star in some distant past. Even if that star is no longer shining, we see its offspring illuminating our sky. We receive the entirety of life in just a moment. The richest moment of all, and it is happening right now within the eyes of the perceiver.

The Universe is vibration.

The Universe is a dance of light, sound and space. It is the combination of these elements that evokes our whole, sublime, ancient self to emerge through all the layers of identity we hide beneath.

When the realm of thought falls away, a nameless essence arises within.

That sacred, transcended space is the home of the timeless being. The unborn self.

We habitually seek outside of ourselves the things that will enable us to merge with the powerful self we project outwardly. We lose touch with our True Self when we believe there ever was a person we were meant to become. We find ourselves again, in the space of stillness. Here, we pause, and notice the eruption of miracles waiting to be seen. We merge effortlessly with our source – the energy that is so all-pervasive it seems passive to the seeker, yet all-powerful to the one who no longer seeks. She is found within herself, and that perfectly awakened essence is not something to grasp or capture, but rather a perfect eternal space in which we can only arrive in the ever-present now.

Chapter 8

The Great Awakening

Origins

Once upon a time, nearly 14 billion years ago, every particle of the Universe was condensed into one point of infinite mass within an eternal moment of compressed time. There existed only a gravitational singularity. In other words, Oneness. Space and time were not things yet. This Oneness could not know itself. It had no perspective of itself, for without space, without light, without reference points, its eyes were blind. It did not yet exist beyond a cocoon, the entire cosmos suspended as an egg inside the dark womb of creation. At the great spark of expansion, the point we call the Big Bang, this cosmic egg hatched. The Universe was born through fragmentation. Suddenly there was enlarging space, notions of here and there, of before and after – and an illusion of separation.

Evolution required a splitting of perspectives so consciousness could be realised. And it is only realised in the recognition that we are still together; we are still bound by an infinite connection. The ancient Vedic texts called this great web of interconnectedness Indra's net. Indra is a sky deity (often called King of the Gods) and above his palace is an infinite network of jewels woven around the Earth, with the properties of a hologram. If you look at one jewel (which represents a soul), you see every other jewel and the entire web reflected within it. This penetrating idea of inter-being exists perfectly alongside Michael Talbot's theory of a holographic Universe. Contemporary quantum physics agrees with 2,500-year-old spiritual wisdom. Despite appearances, contrary to our polarised society, we are One. Consciousness has no boundary. When we are still, an empty mind without thoughts of past or future, we can sense that we are expanding as timeless awareness. There is no edge to find around ourselves, or indeed around our Universe. We transcend concepts, unable to remove anything from anything else. Each particle of existence is contained within every other. We occupy these separate bodies so we can see each other, know ourselves, expand and grow. But if we look deeply, we are connected to every other thing in all of creation – from the beginning through the end of time. You and I are right there in that cocoon with all of our ancestors and all of our children.

The Universe must be awakening because we are the Universe and we are awakening. It must be intrinsically conscious because we are conscious. It's all there in the primordial mush of that cocoon.

Humanity has reached a gateway. We have evolved in body, developed in mind, and now we have an opportunity to align with our true being in recognition of our timeless nature, remembering our origin of Oneness. The next leap in evolution is our Big Bang of consciousness. In order to survive our advancing intelligence, we need to awaken to our soul's wisdom. Our time is asking us to consciously evolve by connecting to our divine essence, and in that, connect to All That Is. If we embody this union and acknowledge this unbreakable connection, we can heal our environment, our global challenges, our collective suffering; we can transform and find our wings by connecting to our Earth, to our soul, to each other and, ultimately, to All That Is. These connections can be enhanced through the hara, the heart, the third eye. I can't help but see Indra's jewels reflected in this image of our three diamonds.

When we step into our truth and live from that grounded place, we bring peace and love and healing here. When we consciously acknowledge our inherent connection, the Universe quickens. We bring more light to everyone we meet and every place we travel. Our light expands.

This is why I teach Reiki. It has always been about your spirit, your mind, your wellbeing as a practitioner. It supports us while it fosters an inspiring reverence for life. Compassion is a natural outpouring of the practice. I see it over and over in that very sweet, child-like expression that lights up on my students' faces – that moment of sheer delight as they connect to this mysterious quality of the Universe with their own hands. Most of our worldly challenges could be healed by cultivating this innocent awe for each other as living consciousness and by revering our natural world in all its generosity.

Reverence is the medicine for our time.

Interconnectedness is a portal into this awakened state of wonder; as we embrace the mysterious and seek to nurture the infinite inside, we find the love that never leaves. We can awaken to our inherent connection and experience natural gratitude for life in its many forms.

Teaching a method for hands-on healing in the strange time of social distancing, as we maintained two metres between each person throughout the attunements and practical sessions, has enriched and deepened my understanding of the Reiki practice. It has placed the focus back on our energy and away from our hands. The deepest sessions with clients have always dissolved a sense of the hands as we slip into the field of Oneness together. In that precious remembrance, all healing happens. To be forced to practise without hands because of our spatial restrictions actually creates an awareness of our energetic connection much faster for the group. We can't be distracted by our physicality or rely on senses; we go deeper into the great beyond of ourselves, and this is exactly what Reiki is for. Below the choppy waves of our mind, Reiki aligns us with the depth of our being, the energy of our soul – the True Self. This alignment is where healing happens effortlessly. For the individual and for the whole. Reiki is the primordial consciousness of the Universe. It's our original energy.

The cosmos is within us. We are made of star-stuff. We are a way for the Universe to know itself.

CARL SAGAN

Humane Evolution

During the great pause of 2020, I walked by our local tube station and noticed a prompt outside. 'Is your journey essential?' What a beautiful question. Is what I am doing essential? Is this outward journey required? Could it possibly be the inner voyage that is essential to embark upon now?

I often use the psychology of human evolution on courses to illustrate the chakras. In terms of our current paradigm, our species has been expressing itself precisely from the solar plexus. The tendency to be masculine, wilful, operating separately from nature as if we are in some sort of race to conquer life, preoccupied with our productivity, actions and identity. Our next leap is moving into the heart. The way of connection, unity, cooperation, kindness, compassion. Feeling and being over thinking and doing. Our perspective is invited to rise from ego to soul. Our identities are shifting in the collective sigh. We don't know who we will be as a human race after this transition, but we are now able to heal the broken bones in our collective body. We are midwives for the awakening world. As we rise again to the solar plexus and revisit the energy we operated from with new eyes, we are asked to continue opening beyond what we've known, to see ourselves as a collective of beings, connected to the natural world that surrounds us and governs our existence. Will we love each other and our Earth? Will we take care of this world as ourselves? How can we keep opening our heart to find this sweeter space of our evolutionary journey?

Evolving into the Age of Aquarius

As we are, human beings have evolved from our infancy into our adolescence. We are teenagers who, by design and complete appropriateness, moved away from our mother to find our identity in the world. This is the realm of the solar plexus – the seat of ego. We have been living in a time of patriarchal energies, allowing male dominance over feminine dominion. Our task, as we evolve into the awakened age of Aquarius – as it has famously been predicted by the ancients – is to move into the embracive nature of the heart. As young adults, after the great exodus from our family, we return home to connect again as the mostly formed individual. The path away from home and family was educational and often challenging. We learned about ourselves through this outward movement of individualism, but we forgot our roots. Now we remember again as we rise into the heart's expansive, all-inclusive energy. We are forgiven for forgetting in the realm of forgetfulness. The soul is always there in unconditional love. We are embraced as we enter our home. We come together again, wiser for the experience.

We awaken to the heart by connecting. Using the simple meditation from 'The Medium Between My Soul and Life' (p.115-116) allows us to see the elements alive in our body. We feel the connection we have to our shared ancestry of light. We can feel the part of us that was once the seed of the Universe as we sit deeply within connectedness. This profound practice is enough to move us all into the heart.

We come home to ourselves *as* the home and awaken to our inherent connection to all of life. We *are* life. We can rise out of the dualistic dream of discrimination, out of complexes that keep us apart, and live in reverence for each other as life itself.

> We are divinity,
> here to know itself as divine.

Isn't it interesting that the Latin etymology of the word *Co* means 'together', while *Vid* means 'seeing'? The virus moved all of society at once, back to the root where healing begins. The first phase included our family, home, routines, habits, inherited wounds and all of those things that support our survival yet are frequently taken for granted. What happens when we all take pause to heal the root chakra? Can we make kindness the basis of our actions?

From the space of our soul we can sense arising compassion for our inherited suffering. We rise like a lotus out of the mud. We can embody a state of being that longs for connection over safety, realising that true connection is our safety. It is no wonder we find ourselves on this verge – the cusp of a primitive collective consciousness as it evolves to its next stage. In our year of perfect vision (20:20), coronavirus arrived as an unforgiving Zen teacher showing us this very lesson. We've confronted our global Oneness. How do we respond?

As we walk upon our planet, we can shift our mental awareness far out of our head and into our feet. As we feel the energy of our feet and pay close attention to each movement of our body upon this sacred land, we can kiss the Earth with each step. We offer immense healing energy with our presence, and she kisses us back with the wind on our cheeks. We show her our love and our gratitude in this gentleness, and as we all begin to move in this grounded way of grace, we come home to each other in the heart. We arrive in the home that we are, together, as a human family.

The Soul is a Flame

Within your soul is an alchemical fire that burns away the illusion of duality. It burns away all untruths as you approach it. This flame is within every single human being. It's alive within the communal heart – you can touch upon it in times of uproar. A collective moment of adversity is often at the cusp of evolutionary movement. Challenges are always found at the crest of the wave, holding immense momentum to pull humanity's consciousness into a far truer space.

The soul is a fire that purifies.

When we step closer to it, the parts of our life that were created when ignoring our intuition become apparent and burn away. Our soul desires to be on this Earth; that is why we are here. Your soul desires to be you, this human being, fulfilled when wholly in-body. Our job is to ground its larger-than-life energy onto the Earth by concentrating on our strong foundations as the base of our pyramid. The soul expresses itself here, yet always pointing to the space from which it came. Everything the soul does is in service to the whole. It will always move towards wholeness, kindness, love and expansion.

The soul is like the sun and the body is like the Earth. The soul's light shines upon the body, while it shines elsewhere in all directions. Its power is too great to be contained, yet we can be fully illuminated by soul energy while in this body. It radiates from within. This is the greatest protection we could ever hope for. Students always ask about protection when learning to work with energy, perceiving their empathy as a weakness. We are generally still a little fearful, not sure about our power as a light in this world. Does the sun need protecting from all the darkness that surrounds it? It shines and shines; darkness doesn't come close to touching it. Its expansive brightness travels far and illuminates worlds beyond what we can perceive. The light comes from within, leaving no void for interference to impose upon it.

A Wake-up Call

As we collectively move towards our divine inheritance, we are waking up to all the ways humans have acted less than divine. 20:20 was a year of culmination. We are waking up to what has been suppressed, who has been oppressed and what parts of humanity require our maternal embrace. What goes up must come down, yet what has been pushed down must also rise. We are on the verge of a huge shift. What we think, feel, believe, align with, and act upon, matters. We are called to listen. To be compassionate. To courageously stand for love, as we embody our light, together.

As a mother holds a singular focus when her child's wellbeing is threatened, so too can we mother the human family to which we all belong. On behalf of our sisters, brothers and the very Earth herself. We are being asked to be guardians for all the Earth's children. For Gaia herself. We must take good care of each other. None of us exists as an island. And we are only as strong as our most vulnerable. As we rise to fall in love with the soul, we love the soul in every other. The Great Bright Light in me sees the Great Bright Light in you. That seeing is inevitable.

Ours is not the task of fixing the entire world all at once, but of stretching out to mend the part of the world that is within our reach. One of the most calming and powerful actions you can do to intervene in a stormy world is to stand up and show your soul. Soul on deck shines like gold in dark times. The light of the soul throws sparks, can send up flares, builds signal fires.

CLARISSA PINKOLA ESTÉS

Closing the Chasm

Everything we have experienced as a planet over recent years, though on the surface seemingly independent events, can be distilled down to a foundation where we lost our footing long ago. Division. The manifestation of this seems to be escalating in intensity, taking us to a tipping point where we can finally, maybe, close the chasm. Maybe it's the collapse before the next expanse of our evolution. This dualistic view is the cause of the unfathomable fires we witnessed across the Amazon and Australia, the coronavirus pandemic, the heartbreaking display of violence against the Black community, and even the thing that had so much of our attention for so long here in the UK, but has been completely eclipsed by more recent events: Brexit.

The prevailing cause is living through the lens of us vs them; it manifests as man vs nature, seeing things as black and white, left or right. We have been living in such a dualistic paradigm with an endless list of polarisations. When the reality of two halves is balanced, we get the exquisite harmony of yin and yang. When the halves are grossly unbalanced because one seeks dominion over the other, we experience layers of inequality, oppression, suffering. The *and* becomes *versus*. A world of duality is painful for the soul and we echo what each other says as we shake our heads in frustration; our heart aches because we all know a deeper truth and we long to see that rise to the surface. Every cell in my body knows this is the medicine of our time. The call of our future bellows the harmonising song of unity.

In this process of opening our eyes to clear vision, we are seeing a plethora of wounds surface from the deep, dark underbelly of his-story. It feels as if our generation is purging ancestral traumas while bringing untruths to light in the same way as when we purify. The cleanse that follows an attunement often takes a similar journey. We experience the sweetness of our pure soul energy and in the light that radiates from the True Self, we expose all the areas of our mind that are false. It can be a very painful process if the illumination brings up our most uncomfortable foundations, as we are witnessing now. Humanity's wounds have been repeatedly reopened as we progress through our current timeline, but the wound can finally heal through the power of our collective awareness. With the clarity that follows integration, there is inspired action, change, alchemy and awakening. A shift.

The Nature of Healing

The nature of healing has several intrinsic qualities: it involves vulnerability, authenticity, courage and transformation. It can be unsettling when the light of truth ripples through our lives. It exposes patterns in the tapestry of our reality that are suddenly in the spotlight, as what was unconscious becomes conscious. The revelations can often provoke the stages of grief – all of which are a signal that healing is well underway. In the turmoil of a healing crisis, we are typically made to pause all non-essential activity and rest deeply with ourselves.

Healing is not about getting rid of something we don't like. We only really heal our pain by embracing it. Healing is the journey to becoming whole. Uniting all the severed pieces. This doesn't excuse an oppressor or mean that we allow anyone to be held down. It means we can't create the change in division consciousness by reinforcing the otherness of the other. We are tasked with accelerating now into the consciousness of the heart – towards compassion and togetherness. We are being asked to embrace each other, to really look at ourselves as an organism in need of very deep healing. We are a human family. Where is that healing flowing to, what is the balm? We each have potent medicine to offer the collective once we've come to wholeness in ourselves. We can truly embrace each other as we realise that there is no self. That appears to be the way of completion in our current cycle. The Earth needs us to rise into the heart with her, to be in reverence at the sight of all of her life forms. This happens so effortlessly when we have paused the button of *me* and how we identify ourselves. The heart is where we connect, where we experience non-duality in the vastness of who we really are; it's our bridge. Inside the heart we merge with life. We can embody our True Self, infusing our world with compassion, kindness and love. The heart guides the healing.

How we each endeavour to awaken is our unique quest. It is ours to discover on our individual journeys towards the same home. This is our devotional practice. Let us open our eyes to understanding and open our heart to love as we share the medicine of our presence.

Ancestral Healing

When we have moved to liberate ourselves, we naturally turn around to help others across a terrain we now understand a little better.

As a child I wasn't taught how to handle my emotions, hiding how scared I was around my father during his illness for fear of upsetting him. This early conditioning (which my parents absolutely didn't intend to teach me; they did their best with what their parents unknowingly taught them) created an adult that doesn't express her pain very well. This bred a certain independence and emotional resilience I am grateful for now having, even if I don't want to repeat that with my own child. This is likely why I am so good at being there for people; I've become the person I really needed when I was suffering.

Once we become conscious of why we are the way we are, we are responsible for safeguarding our children from this unwanted inheritance. We demonstrate our healing with our choice of parenting. Rather than teach him to be strong, I'll teach him to be true with willingness to venture into any emotion that surfaces.

I think this is our greatest gift once we have come through the storm and touched the shore. We are whole and empowered to help others. We know it can be done and we are wise to the way.

When we embrace the lost part of ourselves (that bit we often want to cast away in a hurry) we give love to the version of us that suffers. The attention shifts from the cause of suffering on the external, to focusing purely on what we need now, internally. I needed love and support, so now that is what I offer to myself. Arms wide open for all of myself, from the radiant to the murky. The path of healing reveals this again and again.

I accept all parts of myself, returning to wholeness.

It's this same extension of love that humanity needs now. Healing isn't our path to fix what is broken; rather, it reunites the parts that were disconnected with the powerful medicines of awareness and compassion.

This is what is meant by ancestral healing. We don't need to go back down the lineage and into the past. We send the healing forward, and it ripples back as our lineage evolves, conscious of what has come before us with the will to forge a new path. Our ancestors are not apart from us in some faraway realm. They are alive in every cell of our body. As we heal, they heal. As we awaken, so do they.

Happiness

Where I was born, there is a document for the people that outlines the inalienable right to the pursuit of happiness.

The pursuit.

This implies that happiness isn't intrinsic to who we are, but rather an elusive thing we must strive to reach. That's what our collective structures have been built upon – a sort of quasi not-enough-ness that has penetrated our collaborative understanding of life. What if we reframed our idea of this? What if we woke up to ourselves as beings of joy, here to experience love?

How can we pursue what is already alive in every cell of our being?

What if we acknowledge this intrinsic joyfulness in every other?

What would our world look like if we stopped competing for what was inside all along and started to encourage each other?

If we lived more collaboratively, more cooperatively, we could be mutually empowered, inspired and living as joyful essence in form. Not pursuing anything beyond what that joy guided us towards. This could bring harmony to our collective vibration. We might realise that we need a little less to feel quite a bit more. Can we follow our joy rather than pursue happiness? It's such an insightful time; we can view the priorities of our leaders. Are they more concerned with our wellbeing or the bottom line? What motivates them? What motives us?

If you feel lost, or joyless, where are you? Are you able to come home and inhabit yourself, darling one? Joyless minds have come away from themselves, pursuing their happiness as an external fleeting goal, rather than an internal ocean of energy.

> There is a joy within you that can be
> dropped into at any moment.

I'd love to remind you of your worthiness, but how could you not be worthy of knowing your very own intrinsic essence?

What you need is less, not more. Less thinking, less stuff, less distraction – our society has many trappings to avert us from the very thing we are. That very thing we are is all we ever seek. That joy can express itself through all of life. Children can remind us because they haven't forgotten. Joy is available to you as much as you are to it.

Joy pursues life. We've just had it the wrong way around.

Be Still

Be still and listen to the energy that runs deep.

There is a light that burns eternal. That light exists within you; it is you.

Remembering this truth is your greatest work. Reminding others is your greatest gift.

Teach by transmitting your soul's frequency. Demonstrate a quality of stillness that a stone would admire. Listen to the deep well of Source water flowing through your hara. This is the river beneath the river. Once we remember to find it, we always know the way.

There are easy ways, there are peaceful ways, but there are no wrong ways to journey home. Each must carve their own path to the current of light that connects all souls.

To be alive is enough. You are here to live, to experience life and all it holds for you. There is magic in each moment if only you are willing to look. As you give life your attention, it smiles to you. Your soul weaves a pattern through many, many lifetimes. Each one a sacred container for awakening to the depths of you. You are never-ending yet experiencing this most miraculous moment of impermanent humanity.

You are an energy as vast, as sure, as pure, as pervasive as the entire cosmos. You are an unidentifiable colour in the spectrum of Source. Can you feel yourself as the wave upon the infinite sea? A sea containing all currents, all movements, all swells and tides. The sea of All That Is. Waves and frequencies dance in an undulating mass of Oneness experiencing diversity. Where does the teardrop go when it falls into the sea? Its essence remains, yet its form dissolves.

Going Inward

While resting, open your ears to the full range of vibration in the silence. The quiet becomes loud, full, alive. Take this moment to connect with the expanse of your heart. Your soul is found in this space, in the core of you. Feel the steady rhythmic pulse of life. You are attuning to your true frequency.

When you are willing to stop looking for something in thought, you find everything in silence.

GANGAJI

A Prayer for the Collective

This process will activate your sacred connection to All That Is. Use it to harness your remembering, to slip into the intimate embrace of Oneness.

Breathe deeply into your heart. Feel it open, soften; notice how strong it is.

Place your hand on your chest, noticing how the ridge of your high-heart fits perfectly within the groove of your palm. Connect to your heart. This is the throne of your soul. Linger in the vibration of love that emanates here.

This is a portal.

At this threshold you are connected. In that expansive, vast plane of energy lies the heart of all things.

As you breathe in and out, place all of your attention in your heart. Can you feel why it is associated with the element of air? It is spacious. Vast. This is your open door.

We offer a prayer for you to speak here...

Dear Great Spirit,

May we awaken now. May you shine your light even brighter here on our dear planet. May we accept the healing rays of this light into our darkest spaces. May your light illuminate the truth and spark the path of peace for this world and all her people. May your light radiate brightly from within us and may we see it all around us. As we shed layers of fear, we shine brighter. May we shine brighter now.

May we take this time to heal in every which way. In our body, in our family, in our relationship with our sacred Self and with our world. May humanity awaken now to the light within and the light all around. May we feel connected, equal and more concerned for the whole than for ourselves. May we radiate love for the collective and surrender the fear of our small selves. May our leaders operate from a space of compassion with integrity, and may they transcend their motivations towards power and hold the intention for the greater good.

May we see the divine essence in each other. May we release the intoxication of our egoic separateness and embrace each other with open arms. May we see each other as teachers and appreciate the different flavours of life that we offer here. May we all experience a love that only the awakened soul knows how to express.

May I be a source of light and love and healing here. May I articulate the love of my soul clearly with what I write, what I speak and the energy that I share. May I embody this knowing, this limitless compassion and joy. May I experience an overflowing abundance of love all around me. May I unleash my creative potency and honour my courageous voice. May I boldly express my soul's gifts for the betterment of the whole.

May I witness myself as the ocean rather than the wave. May I savour being a temporary but mighty ripple upon this endless sea of spiritual energy. May I feel happy to be all that I am here – unafraid, and with the pure vision of a greater truth in my heart.

May I be a guide to assist others in finding themselves, to allow others to feel the love I know is there. May I lead by demonstrating.

May I be fully present in the here and now. May I be true to my heart and may I remember there is only love, always.

May we remember, may we remember, may we remember.

May I know that I am a light-bringer. I am here to illuminate all parts of myself – that is all parts of the whole, for I see everything as me.

I am not here to be an ember of what is already lit, but to bring light to every shadow. I do this peacefully. Lovingly. Compassionately. I bear the torch in the deepest caves and walk the path of the bright truth, not so others may follow me, but so that they may see this light in themselves reflecting from my bright soul. So their paths may be lit by their inner flame.

I know that darkness is only fear. I see the shadows are just confusion, asking to be loved and made whole. The light I bring is the light of Source energy; it is the All of what we all are. It is found within each and every soul.

This light can never be taken from me; it never goes out and never fades. My work is to remember. In seeking truth and being true to my being, I come home. In waking up I find myself anew. I see the whole world as fresh, innocent, precious and full of love. In this my light shines even brighter.

And so it is!

Chapter 9

Soul Communion

Come Closer

Can you see me? I am the child and the mother.

Drink me in. I'm liquid love. The sweet waters of your healing well.

My presence is the medicine. I am the healing.

Rest in me. Let me embrace the confusion, the upset, the frustration.

I am the electricity that gushes through your meridians.

I'm the ignition.

I am the one you have been waiting for.

I am the changeless, ever-expanding light of soul.

I am the limitless.

I am the highest expression of who she came here to be. I am the indomitable essence of who she is.

I am She Who Is.

I'm the one beneath the surface. The one who never leaves.

I'm the warm energy you sense on those cold nights of pristine darkness, when you catch the enormity of the cosmos. I'm the stillness you feel washing over you in the midst of an ancient forest. I'm what arises to greet your presence. I'm the whisperer within the chambers of your heart. Can you hear me?

I have watched you, darling precious human, marvelling at your growth, your triumphs, your heartbreaks. I have heard the delight of your laughter, always the one listening as you sing to yourself. I have been there when you felt alone, lost and in need of the love that you are. That I am.

I have been here when you looked the other way. When you sought to fill that sore emptiness the forgetting of me creates. I am found in the deep space of that emptiness.

When you remember me, we chant together in sublime harmony with all of creation. We are the inexhaustible disciple of life. Here to express all that we are, have been and ever will be.

I met you in the dark of your mother's womb. I'll be there as we release to the great beyond. I'll hear the last beat of your heart as you let go to my embrace.

I am deathless. Birthless. Ancient. Ageless.

I'm unbreakable. Untouchable. I am everywhere and nowhere.

I reside within every recess of your humanity. Feel my presence. Together we are the quest and the answer.

My desire is to deeply submerge into this beautiful body, befriended, articulated and realised. Embodied.

This is all you have ever searched for; though you may have looked elsewhere, for something you knew-not-what, I was here. I was always here as the magic to unlock. The map and the treasure. I am your majesty. Can you feel your inherent sacredness? I am all that you are.

Come closer.

The Healing Happens

The Ancient Greek word for soul is *psychē*, which also means life, consciousness and the verb *to breathe*. Through the gift of our breath, we can bring our mind home to our body and our soul, becoming more conscious with each inhalation.

Going Inward

Bring your awareness to the gentle rhythm of your breath now. Just noticing without changing, follow the very easy nature of its flow as it journeys in and then out of the body. Noticing how the out breath becomes the in breath. And how the in breath becomes the out breath. Isn't that beautiful?

The breath is the body's closest friend; it has the keys to come and go as it pleases. The fullness of the breath brings deep purification to every cell. When we bring our mind home to the breath, the breath unites us with our body and soul. Breathing in, I feel the essence of life in my breath. Breathing out, I smile to the essence of life. Breathing in, I sense my soul as the breath. Breathing out, I smile to my soul. I don't have to breathe. I don't have to heal.

The breathing happens. The healing
happens. The soul is home. I am home.

I know the soul as the healer. I feel it as currents of energy
bubbling from the depths of the body. As I place my hands
on another, I feel their soul emerging to blend with their
humanity. It seeks partnership with its beloved. In our
communion with its penetrating energy, our cells come alive
through its intoxication with life. The soul is the electricity
that animates our human body. Spiritual. Natural. Energy.
This is Reiki. It moves as the force of all creation. Reiki is
communication between soul and human – the space of
intelligent magic that possesses them both.

Your soul is the master of yourself. Your ascension hasn't
been upwards to a higher space beyond, but rather inwards
to your cavernous heart – the infinite realm of your great
spirit. As we walk the pathway of self-realisation, we realise
there is no self to identify with. Each footstep becomes
fainter as we merge with the All That Is-ness of our truth.
We are emanations of the Great Bright Light. All shadows
are merely projected opposites to point us back to the
light. Suffering is the trigger to awaken and focus again. A
delicious dance of awakening and sleeping, dreaming and
remembering.

Your soul is the ascended master assigned to your life.
You only have to go as far as the cave of your heart to
meet with that master. Your north star isn't outside of you,
light-years in the distance, but rather it shines in you as the
pure extension of the great All. The whole, holiest, wisest
aspect of your inner being – the Source of your inner light.
To find the meeting point with this inner sage, become still

enough to listen. Find your still point by following the next breath.

> Attune yourself in the quiet, wordless
> transmissions.

Nothing longs to be said, yet the moment is ever ripening to receive your presence.

> The soul is found in sweet silence.

The mind casts a net far and wide, fishing the endless sea for itself – for its essential nature. When it surrenders and drops down into the heart, it finally sees what it's been looking for. The whole Universe, alive at once in the hollows of being. We settle here on the vertical dimension; as we drop deep within, consciousness expands in all directions. We breathe and receive ourselves as a vast being, at any moment present, grounded and open to the whole of our soul. Sweetly savouring every morsel of life. Our true home as divine beings is not found on the horizontal axis of one thing after another, it's where the human plane of chronological existence meets the timeless space, and the gateway for coming back to this place is in our souls. There is an anchor right in our very heart. When I find it, I am held. I am warm, I am bathed in a vast spherical space of light and colours which vibrate outside of our visible spectrum. Here is a limitless realm of subtle vibration. I sense movement as fluid, colours and shapes dance in shifting patterns. There is a sense of roundness, of cycles, of being whole – yet always expanding into more vastness. My true identity is me without *me*.

Going Inward

Be still. Breathe. Ground yourself right into your body, rising into the space of your wise and wild soul. Stillness is the compass. Sense that part of you that reveals itself when you stop looking. Go where this energy wants to travel and follow what it beckons you towards in its joyfulness. Its voice is gentle, comforting and inclusive. It has impeccable timing, guiding you from a much higher vantage point to spaces of excitement, ease and stability. This light within you cares deeply for you. You are meant to meet it, to wake up to it, to live in this joyful awareness of it.

Although you appear in earthly form,
your essence is pure consciousness. You
are the fearless guardian of divine light.

R U M I

Dreaming

She dreamed herself into being.

Each time she sleeps, another life plays out. She lands in worlds of form with every possible experience available to her. Here she may sink into deeper levels of dreams, or she can wake up within the dream to complete lucidity.

As she dreams, she encounters nothing but herself. She dresses as oceans, animals, crystals, flowers, humans. She is every face she has ever encountered. She is every blade of grass her feet have walked upon, every cloud floating above her. She lives this dream from every angle, as all the characters in all the roles.

She is the tundra of the lower frequencies and the euphoria of the highest pitch. She is all the tones of the scale. She is all the colours of the prism – the whole spectrum at once. She is not just a facet of the divine but the entirety. She is nothing special; she is no thing at all, yet she is it all – as you. As me. As we. As she. As ecstatic motion.

Your Spirit is Your Guide

There is no being higher, mightier, or closer to Source energy than your very own soul. Your soul is the source of you.

We grow up looking up; as little ones we seek the guidance of our parents, followed by teachers and maybe gurus, or non-physical light-beings (depending on our preference). As we mature, we look to the sky for answers to life's complexities. It is to seemingly greater authorities that we perpetually give away our power. We are not taught to go within. We are not taught to revere the voice inside our chest as the greatest agency. But we should be. That voice was custom-made just for us, our built-in navigation system. We don't need to ask for directions, we just need to learn how to trust what we already know. The soul is the light within that never fades, the guiding light of our life.

> There is no one on Earth more
> deserving than you to receive the love
> of your soul. You are the beloved.
> You are the mystery it believes in.

You are the only one that can embody the light of your soul; you're here to fully inhabit its divine frequency, to learn how to sing its song. Your exclusive job is to be you. No one else can do it. As an incarnate soul inhabiting body mindfully, gently moving upon this Earth as sacredness, your every gesture can celebrate your essence. Every movement an enunciation of your divinity, each moment an opportunity to enliven pleasure.

Soul Song

You meet your soul and learn its unique song by going in, in, in. The nucleus of your heart contains the vortex to your soul – the seed of your awakening and the inner temple where the wisdom-keepers gather. This space is the vessel for alchemy, the fusion of the elements, the beckoning of emergent life and all the lives that have gone before to the great beyond. Your guide was never somewhere out there. Your true home was never meant to be a faraway heaven kept away from you until some future judgement. You could never be unworthy. Heaven is you, as you are – the soul uniting with its human counterpart. You, darling one, right in this very moment.

The soul lives within your depths as the water of your being; it fully expresses itself as the wave of your humanity. The soul rises to this splendour of itself – to live as this wonder known to us as this human you. As you journey into the deepest dimension of yourself, soul arises to greet you. Its satisfaction is seeing your awareness of itself. You are both fulfilled when reuniting.

It seems that you are twin beings – two aspects of a self – yet there is a truth that transcends this notion. A unique soul expressed as a triad – the mind, body, spirit. This triune includes all facets of the brilliance we know as you.

Consciousness within yourself awakens and erupts to envelope everything around you; the expanded being realises itself as everywhere. It has no fixed place. It is found in every cell of life. The Universe is becoming ever vaster in its expansion, yet it doesn't do this like a balloon with a skin; there is not an inside and an outside. The same is true for you. You are the Universe, expanding right along with all of creation.

When we connect to this brilliant luminosity, we might imagine our soul as a flower made of light. What we might be surprised to see in its love for us, is that the soul is the ever-climbing plant, while we, as its impermanent expression, are the magnificent flower of its creation.

The first time you connect to your soul, you'll be so full of awe – taken back with total reverence for this divine being sparkling with celestial light, transmitting bespoke wisdom just for you. You will feel like it's higher than your human self, on a pedestal in another unreachable realm. Your dear ascension companion. It is your human form that your soul honours. It holds you in as much reverence. The feeling of admiration is completely mutual. Your soul wants you to know that incarnating in a human body is a beautiful yet hugely challenging undertaking. You are admired for doing this work so bravely, so persistently, with such bold endurance through this denser realm. This is not a one-way street of devotion; it is a stream flowing in two directions. Your desire to embody your soul and feel its light emanating from your pores is the purpose of your soul in this moment. Smile and welcome your own light to be known to you.

There is no energy beyond your very own soul that is more powerful for you to work with. The movement of your essence through the vessel of your physicality is the most divine energy you can align to. As you become more and more full of yourself in this way, completely embodying your divinity, there is no space for interference. Your fully embodied tone is a crystal-clear healing vibration. There is nothing more holy, more powerful, or more pristine.

Your soul's energy is your unique gift to open. Close your eyes and allow it to be revealed.

I Am

I am a wave moving through the ocean of the infinite.

I am a drop in the eternal sea.

I am all that is and ever will be.

The Central Sun

As I walked in the park purring at the sun's hot rays on my face, I noticed a row of people sitting on benches, softly smiling with eyes closed, welcoming those same waves of solar energy into their being. They seemed content to do nothing but absorb the joy each of those sun rays contained.

That sun is always shining. Not a second goes by where it thinks, 'I've given enough.' It never stops being a source of light and warmth, and life itself. It's the yang, the seed, and the Earth is the yin, the receptive container for all of this marvellous growth.

Nature teaches us everything we need to know.

We live on this planet experiencing dark days of cloud cover and long cold winters where we've turned away from the light, but no matter how tilted we are in the other direction, that sun is always shining. There is always light. Even in the belly of our dear Earth, she contains a central sun that constantly churns with heat believed to be as mighty as a star.

Our soul is the same as that sunshine. Our source of energy is also found within ourselves; deep in our very core there is a cauldron of infinite light. That same powerful light is ever shining from within you, warming the world around you, illuminating life around you. It is always there. It cannot be destroyed. This light is what you are.

You may thank Spirit, as I have done, when something wonderful blesses your life. It might be the way you end prayers; it's always been the way I have wrapped up my requests from the Universe – 'Thank you, Spirit.' Yet only recently it occurred to me, I have been thanking *my* spirit. The indwelling spirit, which is a spark of the divine essence we all are. This is not an unreachable deity of immeasurable size, not even as the blanket term I've always used to replace the more masculine sounding God, but Spirit is me, *as* me. Thanking Spirit is saying, 'Thank you, pure me.' Thank you to the purest essence that I am – the spark of the one soul, the purest light inside of me that is unborn, unmanifest, uncreated, unlimited pure cosmic potential. I invite you to try this next time you pray and feel how close you are to the eternal Spirit we all are. It resides deep within every part of you.

Cyclic Nature

We are cyclic beings – our lives, our seasons, our soul's lives, all moving through darkness to light and back. We ebb and flow through dreaming and wakefulness. This is our nature as much as the nature of the Universe. We only need to look up to notice the sky never looks the same way twice. We cannot cling hard enough to retain the enthusiasm of early spring, or grasp hold of wakefulness. We can just pause, enjoy the warmth and let life unfurl. We can be aware and at ease with this, or we can argue. Either way we move from summer to winter and return again.

I always imagined enlightenment was a state we reached and then remained. I've come to recognise it is not in the least bit static, but rather, it's as fluid as the mind. I reach it and then it pulls away as easily as the wave retreats back to sea – and then it happens again, and it is the most delicious way of being in the world. If I think about staying there, it goes. Or rather, I go; it seems I lose my grip on it. Clutching it is like attempting to tighten a fist to hold water. I am the wave moving from the shore. In a somewhat helpless way, my mind drags me off the shore and back into the sea. The awakened ones, modern Buddhas of our time, seem to have transformed irreversibly by that awakened state. I just reach for it again by stilling myself. When I'm perfectly still, I am there. I'm there now when I pause. Just being, taking one breath all the way into my depths. No stressful mental noise trying to talk me into doing. Just a presence breathing. Sitting. Being.

It is only now I can comprehend a people as profound as the Tibetans. As an American kid, I didn't quite understand the peaceful non-violence they demonstrated. It was within my surrounding culture's reactive habit to fight fire with fire, yet Tibetans serve as this incredible symbol of unconditional peace. Even in the flames. A mind at war with itself does not bring peace, even if the battle is for its own sake. The non-violent foundation of Buddhism isn't just expressed on the external, it's an internal practice. Our compassion must extend to ourselves as well as a quality of our mind. When the mind speaks with a voice of compassion, it is truly aligned with soul. With our true nature.

We can choose our own state of being and then offer our compassion to those around us. But it must start with us. A mind enraged is a battle cry for healing. And the medicine is love. This is why self-healing is the most radical act. This is why we are being called to awaken – as individuals who are then able to guide others, at peace with whatever is, with no preconceived outcome.

We Are More Than Our Bodies

Losing the identification as 'little me' propels us into the All – the space, the energy that permeates all things. Reiki. There is unlimited power, endless time there. We may go so far as to catch a glimpse of that long-view picture, unattached to the Earth or humanity's survival because we know it's always working out. We are more than our bodies and the Earth is more than a planet. We are that which cannot be destroyed. We are pure energy. When we view the world with the vantage point of wholeness, we acknowledge what is so intrinsically right about it. This rightness is a powerful influence, generating a reflection of this image in the world. The soul isn't looking to fix, it's holding the vision of what is whole.

Our ego is our identity. The narrative of our personality. We use it to take on roles and act out characters.

We only *know* the truth when we let go of
who we *think* we are.

When we lose ourselves, that is, lose what makes me a *me*, we get a little taste of delicious divine – the state of merging with the Ultimate. We drop out of little me and into the infinite sea. The place of peace. The everything space of nothing at all. I feel more myself when there is less of me exerting myself as a me, my and I. When there is less stuff, less reaching, less on the list of what I think I need to do to be fulfilled. Less going somewhere else. Less thought. Less identification. Less planning. Just stillness. Being the beautiful presence of my essence. That is who I am. I find her when I pause. I arrive to the moment *as* the moment in its completeness.

The Universe loves a paradox. Paradoxes are the golden thread woven through the fabric of reality to point us to the truth. We can be enlightened at any time; just by forgetting who we think we are, we remember.

The Soul Longs to Be Human

Dear Heart,

I longed to be you. To be here, in this moment, at this time, awake to all the majesty of life. To be with you, watching you from within, witnessing your growth, your fumbling, your finding.

To be here waiting for you to remember me, to align your mind to mine, to find your heart in me. I have loved you long before we arrived on this Earth. I made plans and maps and special arrangements to journey here, through this divine unfolding, together as one – as this human, as this you. To say we are one implies we are somehow able to be two, counted apart from another, but only language makes it so.

You are the face I see reflected back to me wherever we go. In every mirror, every pair of eyes, every flower, every landscape, every moment of beauty is an expression of our existence.

I love you.

I love being you. Here. Just as you are right now, in all that you have been and in all that you will be. This continuum of you is pure magic to behold. You are my beloved. The one I wanted most of all. The one I cherish most of all.

Your love for every other is a glimmer of the love I have for you. Dear one, you are my pure expression. My dear human. You are life.

Activation

This is a time of global transformation. It requires intense focus on the light.

This is an activation.

Within you is a vortex. A portal to anything that you desire. A portal to an awakened world.

Embedded within your mind's eye is the egg of creation and with it, pure potentiality. Here waits the unborn, the unmanifest. You incubate this egg with your focus on loving kindness and openness.

Embody love. This is who you are. Give it generously. Feel how it moves through you rather than comes from you. See how you cannot give without being replenished. Keep your heart open. You foster openness by listening to your soul's whispers through presence, playfulness, meditation and creativity.

Feel your way there; you can't think your way. In your pure state of consciousness, the egg hatches.

This is your ancient, wise sage of a self.

We can connect deeply without words. Seeing each other as the real divine essence behind the eyes. In this communion you find yourself.

Your heart is your divinity. This gateway is the most important aspect of being human. This is where all lines converge. Work from this space.

The heart is your true home. It is peace. It is love. It is nirvana. The Pure Land.

Thought is interruption. Feeling is connection. The light is a feeling-space.

This is your spirit.

Listen deeply to your soul, to your loved ones, to the world. Listen to silence. Listen to life with all of your attention.

This is your presence.

With this energy you have received an activation.

You have all that you need.

Attunement

And here I am again, communing. I watch as holographic, formless shapes dance, shimmering in front of my closed eyes. They are radiating divine love, holding me in a cocoon of light. And they offer that now to you...

You are a light-bringer. You are here to harness, channel and anchor the divine love of your soul. Your heart is connected to the heart of the Universe.

We see you.

We are holding you in an embrace of love as you bring your light, which is the light of Source, into every corner of your life. We applaud you for your efforts to awaken. Your desire to wake up is aligned with the Universe's yearning to awaken through you. Your soul's longing is the same as the longing of Source. You long for wisdom, understanding and the evolution of consciousness. That is what is happening now, all across your world.

Your beautiful planet is a sacred home that has seen ancestral wisdom and ritual as a well-worn path. Your ancestors were grounded people, deeply in touch with the Earth with everything they did. They knew she was a gift and they stood rooted to her as a platform to worship the divine.

That remembrance comes over your entire being when you marvel at the stars at night. We are speaking today on a new moon just before the winter solstice, the longest, darkest night of the year. The stars will be at their brightest in that blanket of darkness. You too are those brilliant stars, dear hearts. You shine regardless of how dark your surroundings seem.

We see you illuminating all points of consciousness as you expand and evolve. We invite you to enjoy the process. We see many of you suffering through it needlessly. When you surrender to the flow of the Universe, which is the flow of your own soul's calling, life is so much more enjoyable. When you resist, life seems to torture you. This is your ego clinging for control against the current. If something is being pulled away from you, know that something more beautiful will take its place; as a forest fire flattens an area, it enriches the soil for new growth.

Dear light-bringer, we thank you for your efforts to see life through the open eyes of your soul. To see each other with those eyes of compassion and love, with an eagerness to connect. Your soul's origin is a sea of consciousness, an ocean of luminous energy. Your true home is a lustrous expanse of electric connectivity and love. As you embark on your journey to embody a human form, you encounter false ideas of fear. You may have forgotten your rightful inheritance as a being of the light, yet within your heart remains the temple of your soul. Here is a space untouched by this world; it is a safe, warm womb of infinite becoming.

The higher up you travel, the deeper down you go, the more connected things seem – the less dense, the softer, the more blending of energy is felt. We ask you to take this awareness of the coalescing, of the love, of the interconnectedness into your body. Live with a quantum understanding of the formless while in your beautiful form. Travel through life with your two feet on the Earth, but with your awareness in the blending with All That Is. You have evolved in body and mind and soul, and now we ask that these come together – to bring the full illumination of your soul into your world. This is what the planet is yearning for. You do this by slowing down, connecting, coming into still presence and with practice. You do this by putting your attention into your heart, that inner sanctuary with permanently open doors.

Your body is a temple. You have heard this before, but have you considered its true meaning? A temple is a house of worship. Your soul worships life through this temple you call body. The altar, your heart. Lay down flowers and kneel here. This is a place for communion; here there is a holy seat for your spirit. You are a palace of almighty devotion.

Kneeling at the altar of your heart, drink the sweet essence of your truth as you take communion with your soul. Bow in devotion to your light. This is the meeting place of the sacred self, a ritual of remembrance. You have access to the altar at any time; you find it in the still sweet silence, held by the wisdom of nature as you go inward. Close your eyes and sink into your heart. Can you feel that wellspring of energy gushing into the recesses of your mind? This practice will heal you. Making a pilgrimage within will awaken you. You contain a portal to the entire cosmos here, an infinite realm of love. The Universe as one song, melodies formed and not yet expressed. Verses upon verses. All is vibration. All is energy – waves of light and sound. Will you allow your mind to open to enchantment with the Universe, or will you keep it fixated in the limited realm of duality?

Find that peace, even when your mind is busy chattering away with false ideas. You can hold the space for your mind as if it is a person you are kindly listening to. You can listen with deep presence and hold space for that person that suffers. Your space is full of love. This is the soul's space. As you hold this space of love, your pain is healed, suffering dissolves and fear washes away with the power of unbounded truth.

Within you exists an infinite sphere of timeless awareness. This place has never known fear. It has never felt alone in the dark. This is a vast, borderless space where it is always the eternal now. Here there is radiance – light blending with light in a sea of limitless possibility. This realm of the infinite is found within the sacred chamber of your heart. Dearest light-bringer, it is here that the path has led you and where this guide will leave you. It is here that we reside, it is here that you are home. Here is your warm abode within. We extend our welcoming excitement to meet you at this entryway.

Living from this awareness is the key to everything you seek. Peace in the face of war, love that knows of no condition that it should not be freely given, a joy for life itself. This is the source of your invincible summer. This is the cauldron that brews all the magic you long to encounter. It is here you may nurture the seedlings of those wild desires of your soul. This is the destination of your beckoning heart. This fluid Oneness is found within you; once discovered, you will never lose it again. You've been spiritually hungry, craving connection – a place to belong, to be seen and loved just because. Those desires are finally satiated here; they were inside all along. Reside here and move in the world, shining this revelation from your bright, open eyes. Your love is the medicine that heals. Your light blazes the trail for this next leap in evolution.

You are divine consciousness on legs.

We want to thank you, dearest soul. Thank you for sharing this journey with us. You are an extension of us, we are extensions of you and we are infinitely connected just as we are all eternally connected to the heart of the Universe. Your heart, our heart, and the heart of All beat as one.

Resources

Go Deeper

If you'd like to join me for Reiki training, mentoring, or one-to-one healing sessions, visit www.London-Reiki.com

Meditate

To listen to the guided meditations throughout this book, visit www.the-reiki-way.com/extras. You'll also find a collection of online resources, playlists, and videos I think you'll enjoy.

Connect

www.London-Reiki.com or find me on Instagram @brighitta

Share

Please share your insights and inspirations from the book – I'd love to see what's coming to light for you! Use the hashtag #thereikiwaybook and tag me @brighitta so we can connect. Thank you!

Gratitude

Thank you to my husband, Matt, for always telling me like it is and being so real with me. Thank you for believing in me, for all of your beautiful support over the years and not least of all for co-creating the most magnificent space for me to share the magic from. You are the most creative soul I know. I love you so much.

Thank you to my amazingly supportive mum, Anna, for always believing in me and for reading the many many *many* early versions of this book as if each time was the first. You are such a treasure to me! Thank you to my beloved father, Ernst, who has been sending me love from up above whenever I am most in need of your grounded reassurance. I love you both immensely.

Thank you to my sweet lady-loves Claire Horton, Genevra Jolie, Val Flynn, Jasmin Harsono, Rebecca Sherab and Sophie Osborn for sharing your hearts and your generous ears with me while cheering me on. I love you to the moon and back.

Thank you to Kelly for being the amazing catalyst you were on my path and for opening the two most pivotal portals for me (both Reiki and London).

Thank you to every courageous, beautiful soul that has joined me for a course or session; it was your energy, enthusiasm and insightful questions that inspired so much of this book. Thank you for sharing your heartfelt journey with me and supporting my work. An extra special love-wrapped thank you to Ariane, Katja, Korina, Natalie, Cristina, Ayesha, Janine, Jessica, Rachael, Maria, Laura, Duddi and Hannah.

A very big thank you to Frans Stiene for being the teacher I had been looking for from the start. Your dedication to transmit the original essence of the Reiki tradition has been such a deepening resource. Thank you for writing the Foreword with such joy! I have deep admiration and gratitude for all that you do.

Big love to Lisa Lister, the generous, sisterly, wise, witchy, insightful, honest and encouraging soul, for editing the manuscript with such love and for being the most amazing creative guide through the mystical ways of the writing process! Knowing you were in such a pivotal role for this project has made my heart sing. Repeatedly. Thank you!

Thank you to the imaginative, intuitive and brilliant Claire Jakstas for creating the cover. I love how your creativity illuminates all it touches. Thank you to sweet Alice Rose for capturing my author photo in such a gentle way. You are pure love. Thank you to all the wonderful people at Troubador that helped give this book wings!

Thank you to the many teachers I've had in this life and to those that have sat next to me as eager students. Thank you to Eckhart Tolle, Byron Katie, Mikao Usui, Torsten Lange, Celeste Woods, Tony Stockwell, Julia Cameron and Thich

Nhat Hanh. Thank you to the mystery in life itself, and to the trees and animals that always whisper their gentle wisdom to all who are willing to listen.

Thank you most of all to my darling son, Eli, who teaches me every day how to love openly, how to live joyously and how to authentically express all that we are as humans. You're my favourite bean. I cherish all the profound things you say with all your innocence. I love you far more than this little paragraph can transmit.

Thank you to dear Mama Earth, for the wild beauty of your being – for holding us all, for teaching us, for nurturing us, for your enduring patience with us, for allowing us the miracle of living upon you.

Finally, thank you **you**, dearest soul, for reading this book. May the magic of your presence light up this world a little brighter for us all! I am so grateful for you. **Big love!**

About the Author

Brighitta is a London-based Reiki teacher and crystal sonic therapist. With a warm heart and big laugh, she guides her students to discover who they truly are through deeply activating experiences. She retrieved most of *The Reiki Way* while taking walks during the great pause of 2020, as whispers on the wind.

The birth of her son in 2015 sparked an inner transformation. This shift led her to leave her career in photography and to create the Awakening Light Reiki School as a platform for exploring the mystery woven through all of life. She shares Reiki as a sacred, accessible and grounded path of awakening with students from all over the world.

Brighitta uses a marriage of ancient Eastern philosophies and soulful ceremony to support her clients on their healing journeys. She's been practising energy healing since 2004 and carries a sensitive understanding of the correlation between the energy body and its reflection through life circumstances. She specialises in translating these codes to help her clients connect the dots, illuminating and healing the root cause of any presenting challenges. She offers one-to-one sessions, professional training, alchemy sound baths, community gatherings, retreats and more.

London-Reiki.com

Instagram @brighitta

 Matador

For exclusive discounts on Matador titles,
sign up to our occasional newsletter at
troubador.co.uk/bookshop